"*The Anarchivist* reveals/revels in our humanity and therein our capacity to create and share knowledge, to empower and be powerful, and even to exist in time—past, present and future."

ELIZABETH MYERS, *Smith College*

"Huth states, 'Archival appraisal is an audacious act.' This book is audacious—it is the writer's reverie on one particular truth as he sees it through the lens of his experience and his portion of knowledge acquired, like records, over time. It is a brave public appraisal of his own ideas—an audacious act."

SARAH R. DEMB, *Harvard University*

"Based on decades in the profession, Huth's thoughtful reflections examine why many engage in the archival endeavor. This book exposes him as a master wordsmith who has distilled the expanse of archivy into approachable essays. Important in his storytelling are the centrality of humans in the record, his interrogations of words and their meanings, and some examples of using archives to navigate the messy world around us."

CLIFF HIGHT, *Kansas State University*

"Having known, collaborated and caroused with Geof for nearly two decades, his words are carefully chosen, not to be pedantic, but to be eloquently explanatory and richly accessible. This slim volume, that delivers insight and wisdom throughout the almost twenty essays, not only provides for engaging reading by those of us in the profession but should be on the reading list of all would-be archivists."

DAN NOONAN, *The Ohio State University*

isbn: 978-1-939901-14-9

Published by AC Books, an imprint of the AC Institute
www.acbooks.org // www.acinstitute.org

Designed By R.A. Hazell

Printed By Maple Press
Distributed by SPD

THE ANARCHIVIST

History, Memory, and Archives

Geof Huth

to Karen, the better archivist

Who gets to have a voice?

Who gets to have an archive?

bell hooks, Talk at a session of the 2017 Archives Leadership Institute (Berea College: Berea, Kentucky, 28 June 2017).

#archivesquotes

Contents

They don't want to seek a usable past.

They want to be a usable past.

Daniel Horowitz Garcia, Plenary (Society of American Archivists, Cleveland, 20 August 2015).

#archivesquotes #SAA15 #storycorps

Foreword

BY TERRY BAXTER

The first time I really got to know Geof, he was in my hotel room swigging bourbon from the bottle before unbuttoning his shirt to exhibit the relatively fresh scar running the length of his breastbone. He had had open heart surgery the year before. In his case, this required cutting through the skin, sawing the sternum in half and using a chest cracker to expose his heart for repair. It must have worked. It's a decade later. The scar is faded. Geof is a grandfather.

I always think of Geof in relation to symbols. I was going to say in relation to words. But I have sat for hours with him in meetings while he drew elaborate fidgetglyphs. These mysterious combinations of lines, curves, arrows and dots have a delightful aesthetic. For Geof, they also serve as symbols, documenting what he observes and providing a means to recall that scene in his own peculiar way.

Even more important to Geof are the symbols we call words. While he often plays with them for sheer entertainment, he mostly manipulates them—both in speech and in print—to convey his thoughts and emotions to a wide variety of audiences. That words are Geof's lifeblood is evidenced by his prolific written output. From published works to performed works to blogs and social media to correspondence.

While he's claimed that he's always been an archivist, I know that he chose this calling in his twenties after considering life as a lexicographer. He had been a persistent anti-archivist until then, destroying most of the records he had created in his youth—journals, correspondence, pictures. But that has changed. When asked about himself, he has said: "you can find [it] in my personal papers. All is on view. Nothing is hidden. I'm someone often very open and also someone considerably hidden." Geof documents all aspects of his life for others to see. "It's what archivists do," he once told me.

So what does it all mean? Geof has written, "I'm in the memory business because my memory is faulty." There is something to that, but I feel his memory business is not focused on nostalgia but on understanding the truth of things. That requires identifying and revealing the connections among past events, current conditions, and possible futures.

You can see archives as symbols, too. As they first developed, they served as substitutionary testimony, tangible and portable representations of events distant in time, space, or both. That essence remains, but in the modern conceptualization of archives, understanding the relationships among contesting stories and how they relate to a truthful understanding of our world is central to archives and archivists. The archivist's duty is to identify those voices that have been hidden from the human narrative and to reveal, and perhaps even promote, them.

Geof is firm in his belief that the role of archivists is managing information, not in writing history. While that may be true, or at least partially true, the fact is that our understanding of the past changes all the time. If more is known about something, its meaning often becomes deeper, richer, more complex, more true. So archivists may not write history, but they purposefully choose and provide the symbols historians construct their tales with.

His Twitter feed claims he is "a writer and archivist, mostly a poet of mixed means." It is out of this wordy amalgam that this volume of archives-related fact and fiction emerged. In it, Geof explores the world of symbol and connection. There are plenty of dilettante writers and thinkers. Geof Huth is not one of them. I have known Geof for some time now and have never seen him approach his work trivially. His creative impulses are aimed at uncovering truths and using those truths to positively impact individual and collective lives.

The power in archives lies in their ability to make us confront the past, even when it is deeply troubling, in order to understand our present realities. This confrontation occurs when archivists fight to include as many people's stories as possible. The communion between the living and the dead is the only way we can heal and grow. Archives are the traces of these conversations. As a physical scar is written on the skin, archives are tangible manifestations of the voices and actions of our ancestors. Geof has said "the heart will tell the head where to go and it will often be right." Geof is writing to crack open our chests, force our hearts to lead our heads to confront our pasts, and to heal ourselves and each other.

On February 3rd of this year, with only a faint whiff of pandemic in the air, Geof posted a pwoermd: *impossiblest*. I read this as impossibly blessed in relation to the impending birth of his grandson, Archer. But as Geof has noted elsewhere "the text is merely itself and will be read differently." So take this work for what it is. Like Geof, it will entertain and inform you, but more importantly it will provide a pathway for healing. Now especially, that is a precious gift.

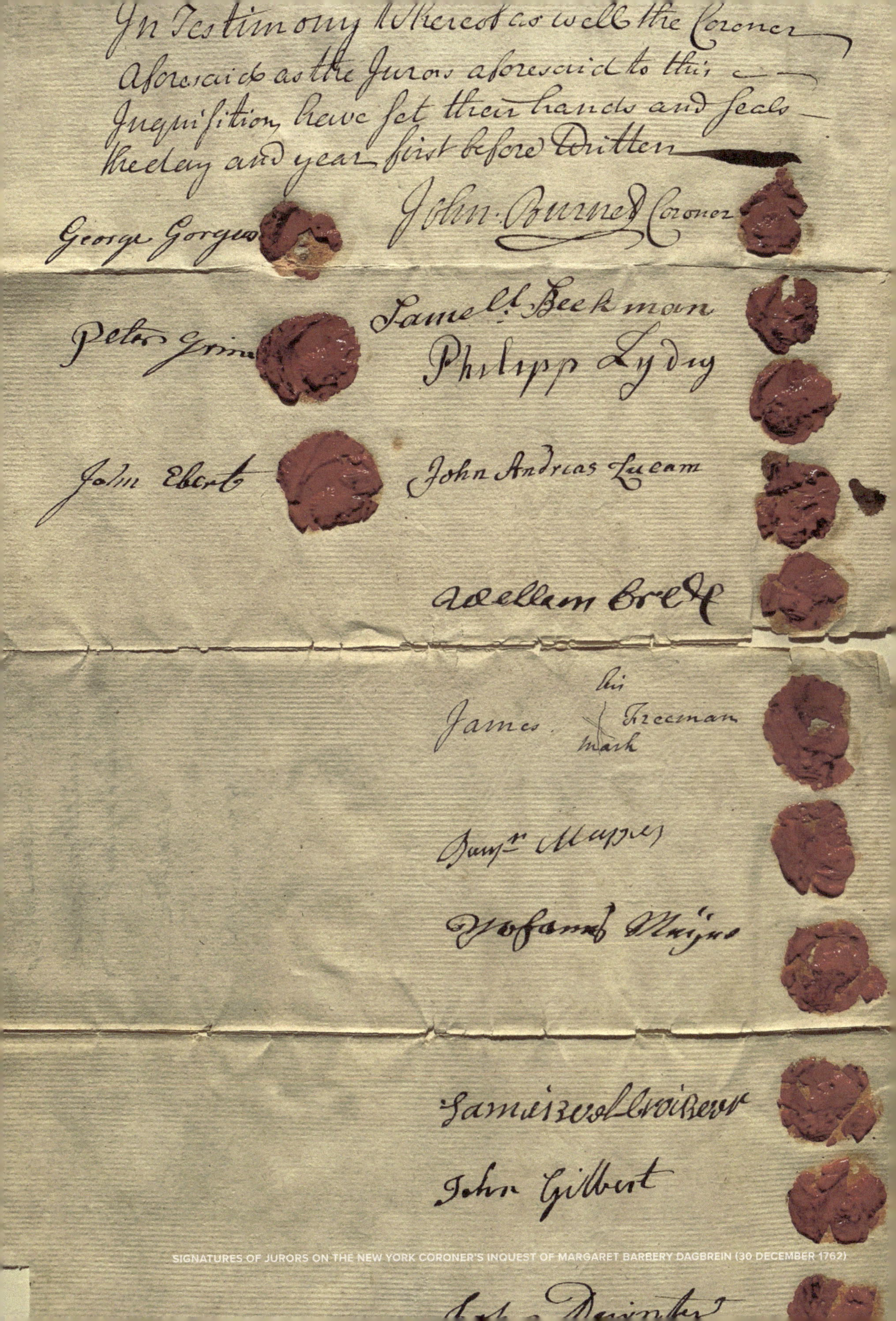

In Testimony whereof as well the Coroner aforesaid as the Jurors aforesaid to this Inquisition have set their hands and seals the day and year first before written

John Burnet Coroner

George Gorges

Peter Grim

Saml. Beekman

Philipp Lydig

John Ebert

John Andreas Lucam

William Crell

James his X mark Freeman

Benjr. Mapes

Johannes Meyer

Samuel [illegible]

John Gilbert

John [illegible]

SIGNATURES OF JURORS ON THE NEW YORK CORONER'S INQUEST OF MARGARET BARBERY DAGBREIN (30 DECEMBER 1762)

The archives, they do bleed.

They bleed our human blood.

Geof Huth, @geofhuth, Twitter (17 August 2018).

#archivesquotes #SAA18

Author's Note

I originally posted most of these essays to my blog, *The Anarchivist*, though two appeared in *The Metropolitan Archivist*, the journal of the Archivists Round Table of Metropolitan New York. Most of the essays here that have appeared on my blog will be suppressed from that space while this volume remains in print.

The title of this book comes from my blog, but I have closed my correspondence with *anarchivist* after my signature beginning sometime around 1992, so it is a word I have associated with myself for decades. Certainly, the term references the word *anarchist*, but more importantly it defines me both as an archivist and not an archivist at all, because I'm also a records manager, a librarian, and (as I hope the book demonstrates) a poet and artist.

I created all the photographs in this book, most of them while working at the New York County Clerk's Division of Old Records, a unit of the New York State Unified Court System, my institution. These records—by their physical aura and their informational richness and complexity—were a major source of inspiration for these essays.

The quotations that appear between these essays were harvested from the series of #ArchivesQuotes I posted to the Twitter feed of *An Archivist's Tale*, a podcast run by my wife, Karen Jamison Trivette, and me.

Thus, even within a pluralist, postmodern perspective, context is taken to be a source of truths—multiple, conflicting, and interwoven as they may be—about the records.

Emily Monks-Leeson, "Archives on the Internet: Representing Contexts and Provenance from Repository to Website," *The American Archivist* 74:1 (Spring/Summer 2011): 45.

#archivesquotes #SAA18

Miniatures (done while in hiding)

Archives are first about the desire to create and finally about the need to keep. Those are its central principles.

My own interest in this field has always been bifurcated, but in a different manner: divided between an interest in the information archives contain (and the use humans can make of them) and the aura they exude, the spirit that animates them and draws us toward them.

I find myself thinking about these issues because in February of 2020 I met Tom Fuchs, a retired businessman living in Palm Beach, Florida, who told me the story of his mother, Valerie Fuchs, the glove designer who created Isotoner gloves. Her papers rest within the Special Collections and College Archives of the Fashion Institute of Technology Library, which my wife, Karen Jamison Trivette, oversees. I accompanied Karen on a trip to meet with donors to the FIT Library and found myself in Palm Beach, about a mile from Mar-a-Lago, talking about this glovemaker.

The story of Valerie that intrigued me was not the one about her success in the glove industry or how she designed and named Isotoner gloves, likely the most famous gloves in the United States. Instead, I was enchanted by a grim story, but one finally transcendent.

In 1938, when she was about 26 years old, Valerie Weil married Leslie Fuchs, likely near Martin, which at the time was part of Czechoslovakia. By the fifteenth of March in the following year, Nazi Germany took control of that entire country. Most of her family was sent to concentration camps, but her husband was held back because the Nazis needed dentists—and for some reason she was spared along with him.[1]

Knowing they would not long survive under the thrall of the Nazis, they found people to help hide them, first in the attic of a villa, then a crawl space used to store wood, and finally an attic in a house.[2] During these years of hiding, those with her entertained themselves sometimes by playing cards,[3] but Valerie did something else. She created. She created elaborate tiny drawings in pencil, always on small pieces of graph paper.

At this point in the story, Tom showed me the drawings[4] on his phone, and I was amazed by their detail and geometrical precision. I could see she began this practice not merely because she loved drawing. She must have made these because the concentration they took would focus her mind and temporarily blot out

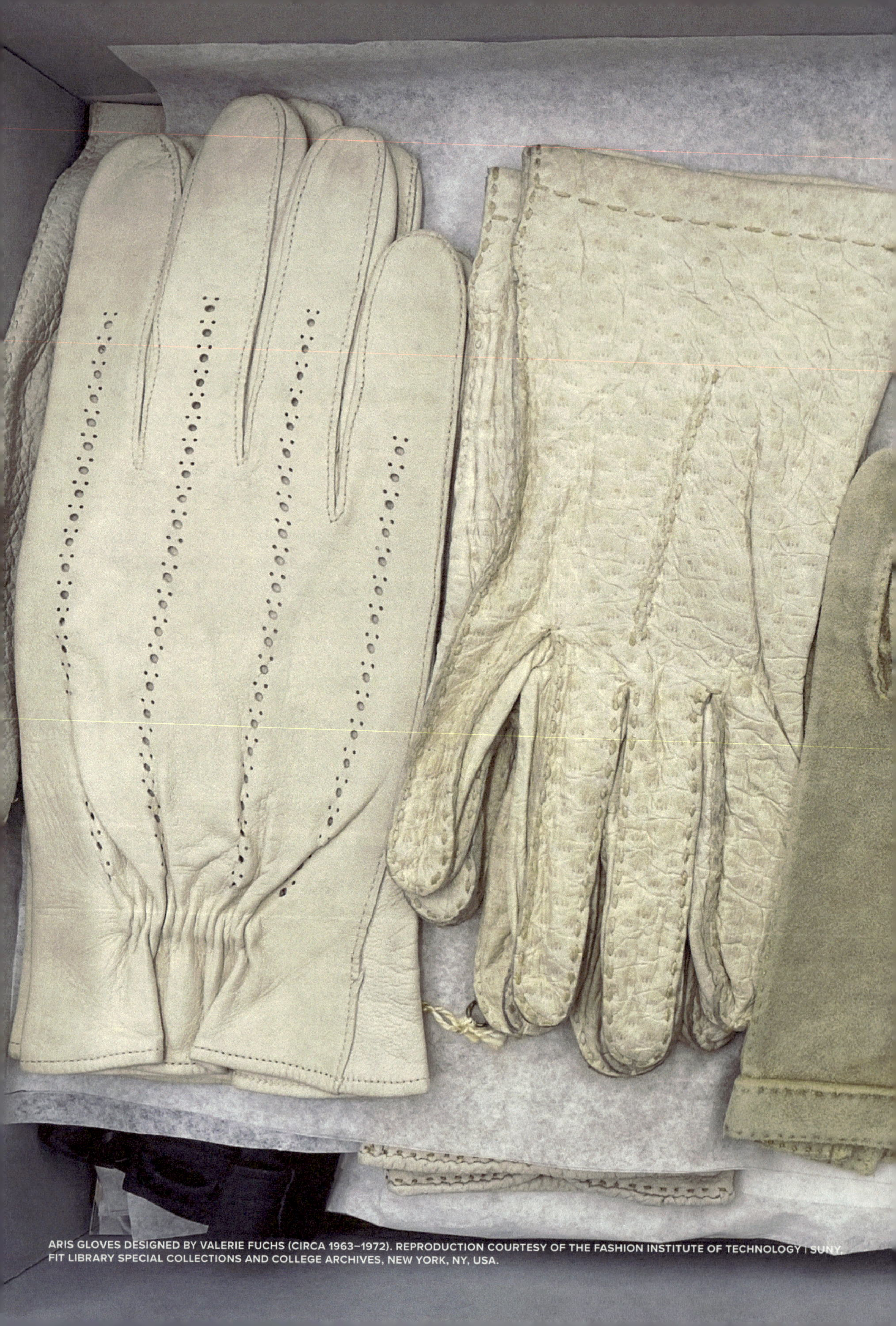

ARIS GLOVES DESIGNED BY VALERIE FUCHS (CIRCA 1963–1972). REPRODUCTION COURTESY OF THE FASHION INSTITUTE OF TECHNOLOGY | SUNY, FIT LIBRARY SPECIAL COLLECTIONS AND COLLEGE ARCHIVES, NEW YORK, NY, USA.

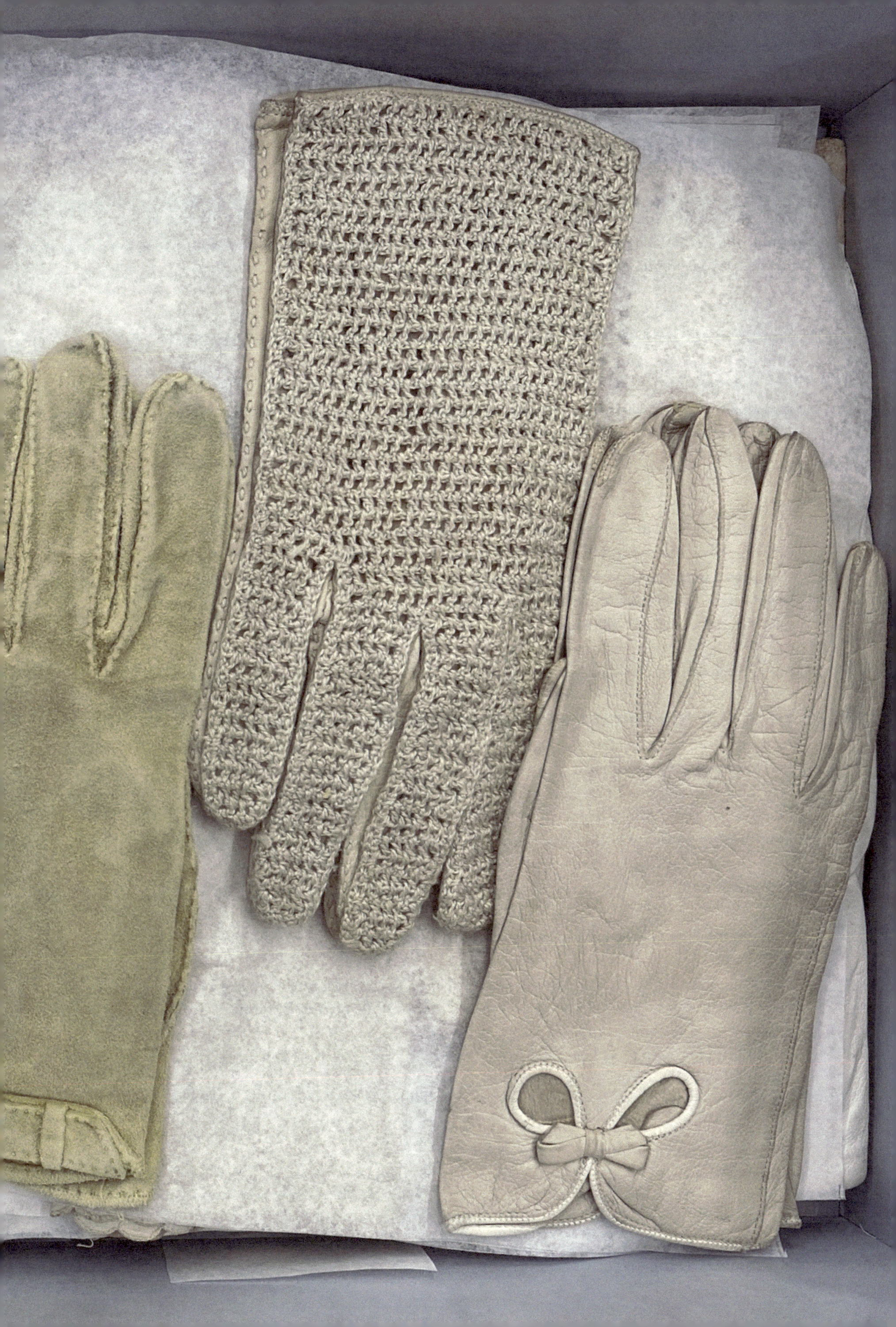

her perilous situation, one she knew might end with her death. By drawing, she could immerse herself into an all-consuming act of concentration.[5]

And she made a record. Not a record of her hiding. Not one of her feelings. But one that was touchstone to the past, showing what she had done while waiting for the day she could fully live again.

She also saved her drawings, which are, by far, the oldest records in her collection. Although they are not dated, she made them sometime from 1939 to 1945. She had to have taken them with her when she left her final attic and escaped into the real world. She must have stowed them in the single bag that held all her possessions.[6] She kept these drawings with her after her only child, Tom, was born. She took them with her when she reunited with her husband in England[7] and when her small family immigrated to America.[8] She held onto them, at least some of them, for the rest of her life.

There is magic in this story, something one cannot know merely by seeing the drawings, but something that the finding aid of the records explains to us, something we can divine, something Tom told me, a critical piece of metadata that reveals the aura of these records. Even if these drawings do not glow for everyone who sees them, they will for many of us and they did for Valerie. To her, these drawings must have represented life—and not just life as survival; they also held the promise of the life she would one day have, the one she was born to create.

The drawings held and still hold within them the promise of the possible, hope for her future while she merely existed in that abbreviated world—a place she had to escape from to ensure she could thrive. The skills she used to make drawings she repurposed to design gloves, and to devise a new world for herself. She lived a good life, a productive life, a meaningful one, and her records hint that hers was filled with love: for her work and her family. Yet she still needed to keep those drawings to remember what she could do, by recalling what she had already done.

I am writing this tiny essay to remind us of the emotional power of archives and the power of people to endure across years of darkness. I am writing from my own little abattoir, sequestered as Karen and I are, in our apartment, in the city of New York, in the middle—I hope the middle, and not merely the beginning—of a coronavirus pandemic that has hit this city hard. We know that at least 14,904 of us are infected with the virus.[9] We know that many more Americans and people across the globe will die from this before it subsides.

So, we hide from the world right now, and we await that day when we can escape this tiny shelter and return back into the big and slightly less dangerous world. I write these words as own tiny archive, my own tiny creation, something I make to remind myself there is something I can still do.

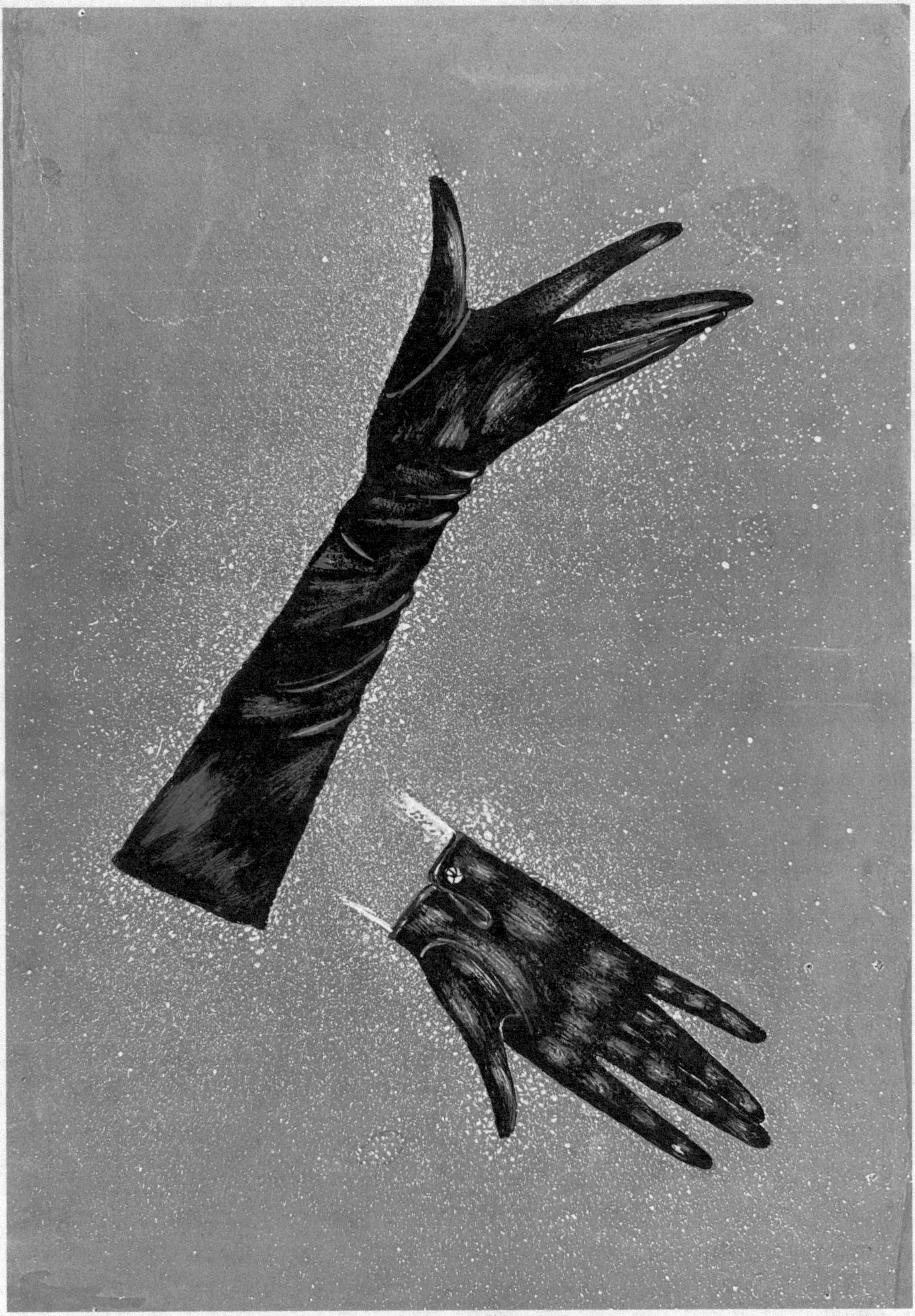

GLOVE ILLUSTRATION BY VALERIE FUCHS (CIRCA 1963–1972). REPRODUCTION COURTESY OF THE FASHION INSTITUTE OF TECHNOLOGY | SUNY, FIT LIBRARY SPECIAL COLLECTIONS AND COLLEGE ARCHIVES, NEW YORK, NY, USA.

History is never the simple repetition of archival content, but a pulling away from it, in which we never stop asking how and why these words came to wash ashore on the manuscript page.

Arlette Farge, *The Allure of the Archives*, translated by Thomas Scott-Railton (New Haven: Yale University Press, 2013): 75.

#archivesquotes

Discovery and the Joy of Uncovering the Unbeknown

We find joy in finding. As humans, the discovery of a new and interesting thing snaps us out of our most natural state of sleepwalking through the necessary routines of life. When we find that thing—something we may have been searching for, but also possibly something we had no idea existed—we become alive. Our minds awake. Our bodies feel the excitement of these discoveries via the beat of our hearts, a sudden intake of breath, horripilation along our forearms.

The thing revealed could be anything. In my own life, such events have included the sight—while hiking out of the deep Adirondack woods in the rain after a weekend of camping—of hundreds and hundreds of salamanders, each a bright but mottled orange, that had emerged from their soft moist burrows to enjoy the cool wet rain. Finding, as boy living in Bolivia, perfectly preserved trilobites resting upon the open ground in the high Andes. And, this week, receiving, as a gift in return for a gift from me, a selection of small poetic broadsheets from Hermetic Press—each of them on different papers, set with different letterpress type, and verbally and visually exotic and appealing.

I was, in none of these cases, the creator of these revelations. I did not set up the world so that I could find these. I happened upon them through the course of the accidents I have come to experience over my life. Others had made these or seen these, and even documented these, before me. Yet they suddenly became shuddering epiphanies for me.

Because I had discovered things I was ravished by.

And I want others to find such things through their own accidental lives. I do not want to deprive them of the joys of their discoveries. I want them to be discoverers, even if only of things already discovered by the rest of us.

So let's think about this in archives terms by starting with a word we have only fairly recently begun to use in a particularly archival sense: *discovery*.[1]

I remember the first time I heard this word used in our particular way. I don't remember the date, but I remember the source. This was a number of years ago, sometime before the 2000s became the 2010s, and happened when I was working at the New York State Archives. Michelle Arpey—who ran our information services unit, which consisted of archivists who developed the information tech-

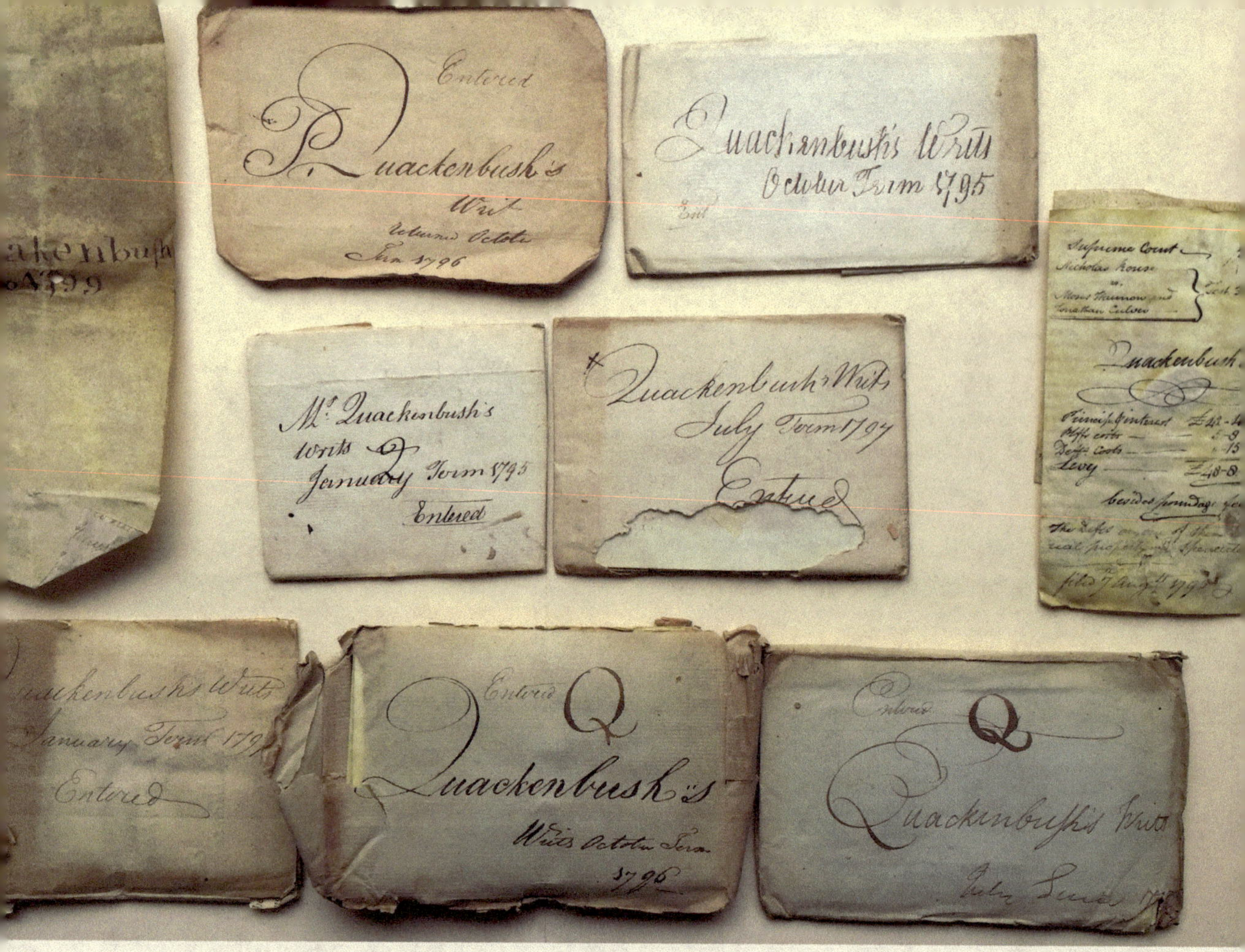

SUPREME COURT OF JUDICATURE WRITS FOR ATTORNEY QUACKENBUSH, 1795–1799[2]

nology that supported our archives and records management services—told me archivists had begun to use the term *discovery* in place of *access* or *finding* or other terms we use for this penumbra of concepts. I loved the term, because it was both active and bold. Our patrons were not just searchers sort of finding kind of interesting stuff; they were intellectual sleuths discovering information new to them—and also, to be sure, sometimes new to the archivist. More on that last clause in a moment.

In my conceptualization of archives,[3] the ultimate purpose of our field is the creation of knowledge.[4] I also see knowledge as a particularly human attribute. People have knowledge. Records don't. Books and archives and even artifacts can concretize and store knowledge, but they cannot *have* it. They cannot know the knowledge that encrusts them. Knowledge, by my thinking, is the primary concern of archivists. We demonstrate this by identifying the recorded knowledge we believe is most important, by making this knowledge easier to discover, and by providing access to that knowledge base through the knowledge we, as humans, create when coming to know the records under our care.

Let me put it this way: Imagine we live in the world of *Fahrenheit 451*. In that world, our only way to preserve recorded knowledge is to store it within this (flawed) storage device we call the human brain. Since it is our only hope to transfer knowledge to the future, we—as a community—carry out this onerous task to protect our collective memory and to ensure our survival as a thinking species. Eventually, we realize that we live in various human communities, large and small, concentrated and dispersed, and that our only purpose is to better the lives of the citizens of these communities (the largest of which we call Earth). In such a world—which is the world we live in—we humans need stores of knowledge that allow us to create eurekas that can better humanity. We cannot depend on recorded knowledge because it is merely potential knowledge. We need the kinetic knowledge[5] of humans, a knowledge which weaves together every bit of information inside a human skull to allow that person's brain to make connections between disparate sets of knowledge that then increase our collective knowledge and better the human family.

That is our purpose. And it is broad and deep and difficult and nearly impossible—so it is what is most worth our effort to achieve.

At this point, we can return to discovery. As we now see, discovery can sometimes be that eureka moment when a person has accumulated enough knowledge and made enough connections among the pieces of that knowledge to make an intellectual breakthrough.[6] And part of that moment of realization is the discovery of that one record they did not know existed or did not believe they would ever find. The archivist might have found it before the user, the archivist might even have been the original finder of the record—but neither of us, not the archivist nor the user, was its creator. The creators, not us latecomers, are those who are important. They are the ones who created the knowledge in their heads and then recorded it. We archivists are interlopers into the world of creation—simply appraisers or considerers. We are only rarely creators of the knowledge we purvey.[7]

Because our roles are not as creators, we also experience the joy of discovery. We discover what others have made—during our process of appraisal or afterwards—and we are amazed by the beauty or insights or value we find within the archives. We experience a spark of joy, and it is joy about something we did not create, but one we connect to. Some of these experiences we expect, such as when we encounter a centrally important document in the papers of a famous writer or scientist we have just accessioned. But some of these experiences are mere surprises. We might open a journal of a nameless woman from the 1800s and find laid out before us a world that has disappeared forever yet rises off the page and into us.

Still, that journal had already existed. The scientist had already written his theorem on string theory. Another archivist had appraised the records—or, in the case of the personal journal, had possibly accepted it without much consideration, utilizing a laissez-faire means of appraisal not too rare in our world.

Because of these two facts—we are not the creators who made the physical or digital objects in our care, and the joy of discovery is part of the allure of archives—we should be considerate when dealing with the cries of "Eureka" emanating from our users, even in the cases of journalists exaggerating the hiddenness of records.

Let's first put this in perspective, in a couple of different ways. I understand and even possess the urge to complain when people say certain things about records. "Never-before-seen" is never true. Never. Somebody has always already seen a record stored in an archives, even if it was only one person, and even if that person is now dead. But to become agitated by this usage is a bit unfair.

When we focus on the falsity of the statement, we ignore the fact that it is not meant literally. We ignore the fact that language itself is often not meant literally,[8] but archivists are usually trained to be literalists, so I can forgive us our tendencies. If we complain about such statements, and then call out journalists for undervaluing our work or making it invisible, we are making pedantic statements, likely coming to false assumptions, and possibly assuming others don't see the value of archivists' work when they actually

SUPREME COURT OF JUDICATURE WRITS OF ERROR BUNDLE (1799)

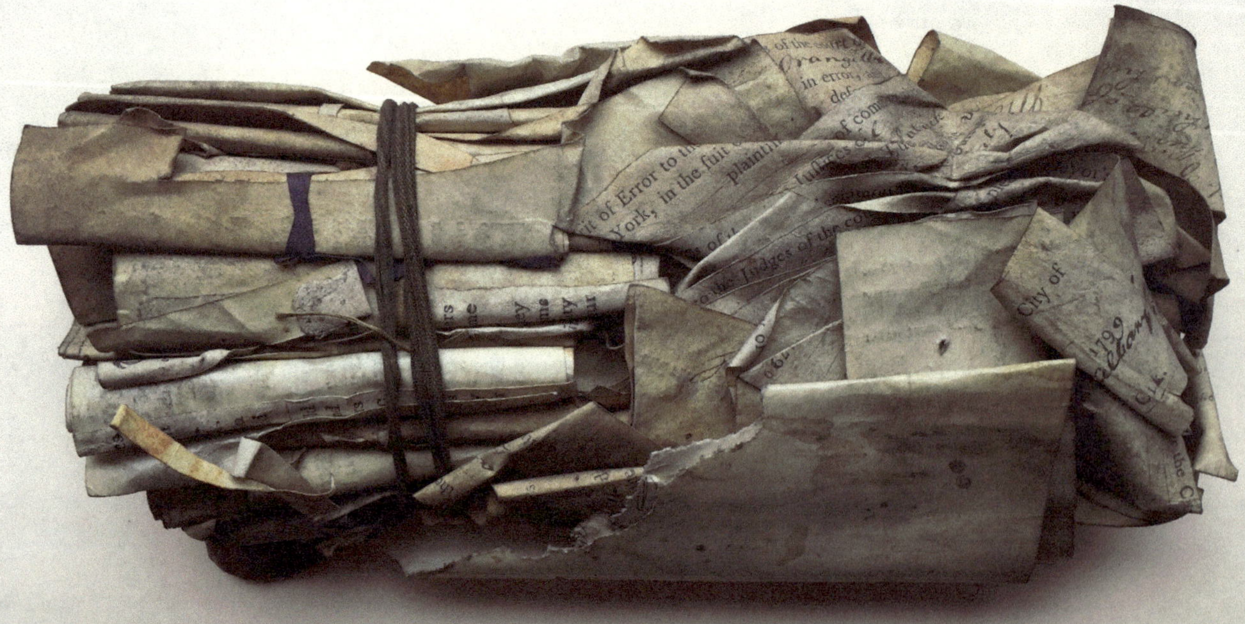

do. I've seen such news articles before, and they do include the occasional panegyric to the archivist.

We also often complain about others calling our archives dusty when they are not, but I work in an archives with a century's worth of dust (an archives I'm slowly moving the mass of elsewhere), and I know of plenty of other dusty archives, so I didn't mind when dust was prominently mentioned in an article about my work.[9] I even embraced that dust, which I discuss in a little article I wrote.[10] So there are ways for us to reorient our perception and thus take vigorous advantage of our opportunities.

But that is the small problem, an issue with perception. The big problem, from my point of view,[11] is that for us to expect users to frame archives as we want them to is unfair to them, for a few reasons.

First, we must be active creators of people's perceptions of us. If we don't help them understand how to perceive us and our work, we cannot hold them responsible for their misreadings. To be fair to non-archivists, archives are arcane sites to most people. Those who visit our archives do not know how the archives had come to be, how we make decisions about what to preserve, or even what we know about the records under our care. So we must be active creators of our own press coverage.

We also must accept that we do not know our holdings in their entirety. In most organizations, we have too many series or collections to know even a little bit about all of them, so we certainly cannot know their entire contents. We never do, and finding aids reveal only the outlines of the records in our care. An archives is always filled with secrets, pieces of information lost to the human storehouse of knowledge because they do not reside in anyone's head anymore, even pieces of information the original appraisal archivist never knew. We know we don't know everything about the records, yet we are concerned when people say they discover surprises among those records. The fact is we ourselves make discoveries in the archives all the time—I certainly do—and we should embrace those discoveries and accept the joy we receive via them.

And we should honor and celebrate the discoveries our users make—even those that are not discoveries to us personally. We should do this because they are still discoveries and because we want our patrons to experience joy as they extend their knowledge. And we should do this because we are servants of people, which I tell my staff is the highest calling anyone can accept. It is good and honorable and potentially[12] joyful to serve people, and if we allow them the joy of their discoveries they will return the favor to us.

The pervading view of archives as sites of historical truth is at best outdated, and at worst inherently dangerous.

Elizabeth Kaplan, "We Are What We Collect, We Collect What We Are," *The American Archivist* 63:1 (Spring/Summer 2000): 147.

#archivesquotes

Dirt

We dream of brightness, cleanliness, dustlessness—and many of us operate in such places. Archivists in those archives clean them periodically, monitor and manage their temperature and humidity, and ensure access controls protect the records from natural disaster and the ill intent of humans. But I have rarely worked in such spaces. The archives I've inhabited have, almost universally, been somewhat dirty and chaotic.

Maybe this is because I have rarely been a pure archivist. I have worked in significant archives—the New York State Archives and the special collections and archives at the University at Albany (before it gained the name "M.E. Grenander")—but only occasionally have I worked in an archives—and when I did, it usually wasn't clean.[1] Most of my work at the university was field work: I visited unions across New York's greater capital district, examined their records, and encouraged them to donate archival records to us so we could add them to our labor history collection. The storage for many of these records was reasonable, but I also found damp records in basements of union halls and personal homes, and I found dirt.

My positions at the state archives focused on helping local governments manage their records, whether archival or not. The usually small records storage areas I visited were—at the beginning of our work with them—in disarray and disorder, dirty, damp, and dusty. Records storage areas were sometimes so full that a human being could not enter them without first emptying boxes from the room to create a path into it. I've visited towns that stored official records on the bare earth of their barns, which in one case destroyed, with colorful florid mold, the town's earliest minute book—and thus its earliest record. In one town, the records were stored in the dry floor of the basement, while the floor was ringed, in its entirety, by a moat about a foot wide and 18 inches deep filled, constantly, with water. Records stored in town garages were always covered with the sticky sooty blackness of accumulated exhaust. A town in the Adirondacks stored its inactive records, no matter their value, in a small wooden room covered with a roof only partially protected with roofing tiles. In one case, a suburban town had to address a storage attic after discovering a raccoon had been nesting within it.

In attic or attic-adjacent storage, the occasional dead pigeon or bat was a common sight. And one city in the state stored a good portion of its records in a giant hole dug into the soil in the basement.

What I've learned about dirt and dust is they are merely part of the natural process of entropy in any paper recordkeeping system. Insofar as archivists dispel dirt and maintain order, they hold the natural process of disorder at bay. A single scrap of paper not lifted off the floor, an individual document not returned to its specified location after use, the passage of enough time to allow dust to become visible on a shelf—all of these initiate a movement toward disorder, one that will continue through the also natural process of inertia unless the archivist counteracts the direction of that inertia. To keep a place clean and orderly, one needs action but one needs more importantly the rhythm of routine. We can accomplish even a despised task if the process of regular routine makes it natural to us, allows us to carry out the task without thought, in a state of blank meditativeness—which is how we make an act inertial.

The presence of a bright, clean archives is part of the evidence of the archivist's work and value. We are proud of the sterile appearance of our archives and the physical perfection of the arrangement of boxes upon shelves. When a user opens a box of ours and sees a sequence of crisp folder tabs labeled neatly and cogently in pencil, we realize our work is visible because they see it. This explains why archivists decry references to archives as "dusty," while sometimes even decrying that archives are never dusty, dark, or dirty—even though they occasionally are.

Order is evidence of the work of the archivist. Disorder is evidence of the lack of an archivist.

Or so we desire it would be.

Truth is I have worked with many messy archivists, too. I am relatively neat, but I can allow disorder to invade and overtake my work spaces. Lack of time, more than lack of will, may be the cause of this, but an incomplete willingness to act promptly is still a cause of my disorder. I shared an office once with a great archivist, friend, and man who had no ability to keep a tidy office. After he opened an envelope to read a letter,[2] he would drop the envelope onto the floor—despite my entreaties that he use a trash bin instead. By the time he retired—and this is not an exaggeration—the floor of his office was almost a foot deep with paper, except for a narrow pathway to his desk and enough space to allow him to operate his rolling chair relatively unimpeded.

Yet such personal habits of archivists in their own spaces is not of crucial concern to us. It does not matter how we manage our own affairs. What matters is how

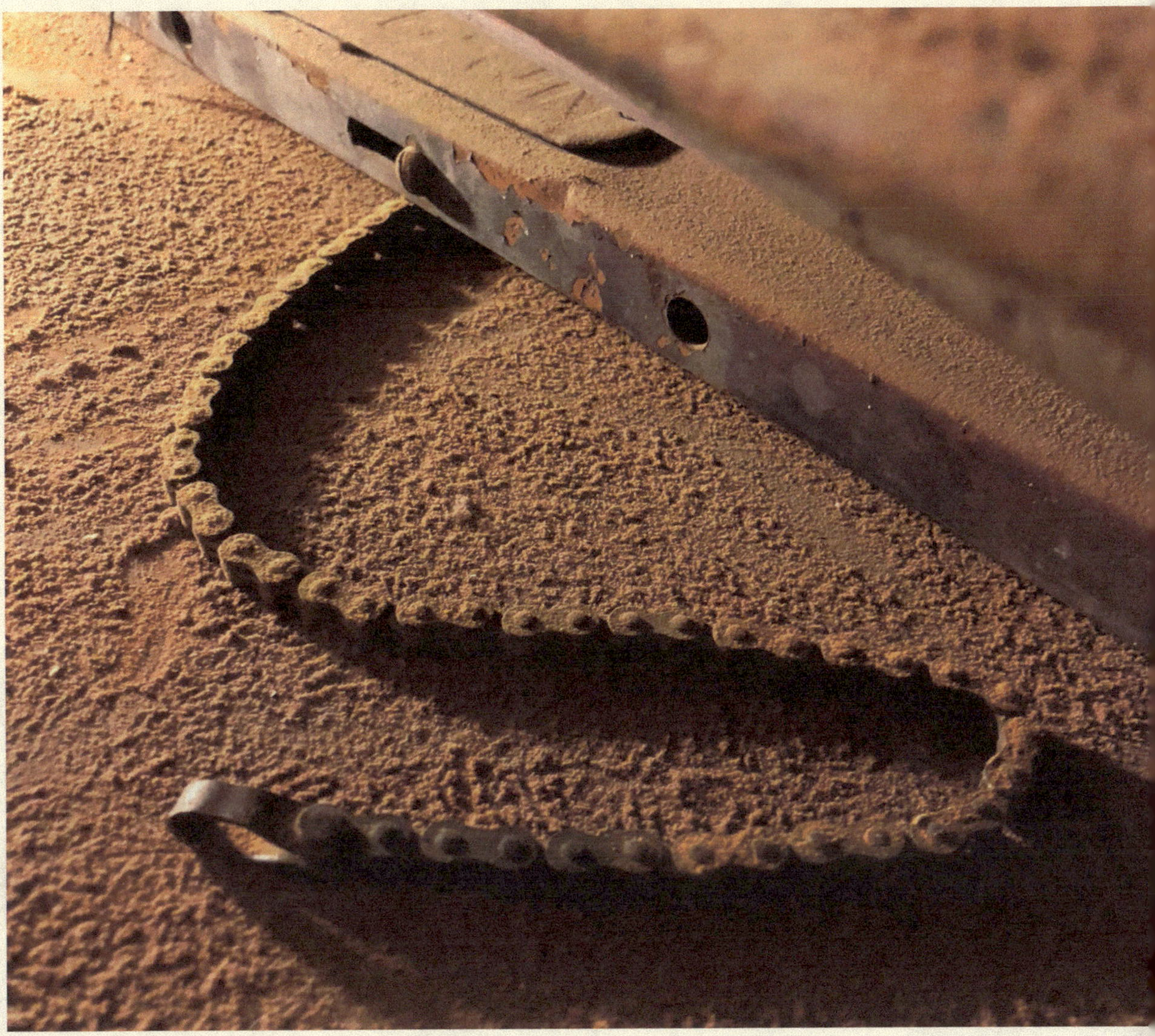

DUST ATOP RECORDS STORAGE SHELVING IN THE ARCHIVES (2018-05-01)

we manage the archives: the records, the space, and the organization. Our profession extols order—and not just physical order. We require controls to protect the archives and make them discoverable and knowable. We restrict access to storage areas. We require users to follow certain rules that protect the records, because protecting the records ensures their survival and continuing re-use.

Order is our guiding principle. Even if good order is not one of our personal habits, it remains our defining characteristic. So when I'm working in the dirty archives where I now work for part of my time,[3] I struggle towards order and cleanliness. Thousands—and I mean thousands—of bundles of records were stored on open shelves but wrapped in canvas-and-pine Willis files that exposed their tops to the indoor elements: primarily dust, but the occasional drip of water or dead moth. Now—after much work by staff in my office—these folded documents rest in labeled boxes, most of their disorder undone. (However, probably over 1,000 cubic feet of such bundles sit in the relative security of Woodruff file drawers, awaiting us to begin to rehouse them.)

When we began our efforts in our dirty archives, parts of many series were dispersed across our space—and even across various floors of the building. We have brought series back together, described about 1,000 cubic feet of those, and cleaned away the dirt encumbering them. We are cleaning as we proceed: mostly by HEPA-vacuuming before we box the papers. But I've cleaned the tops

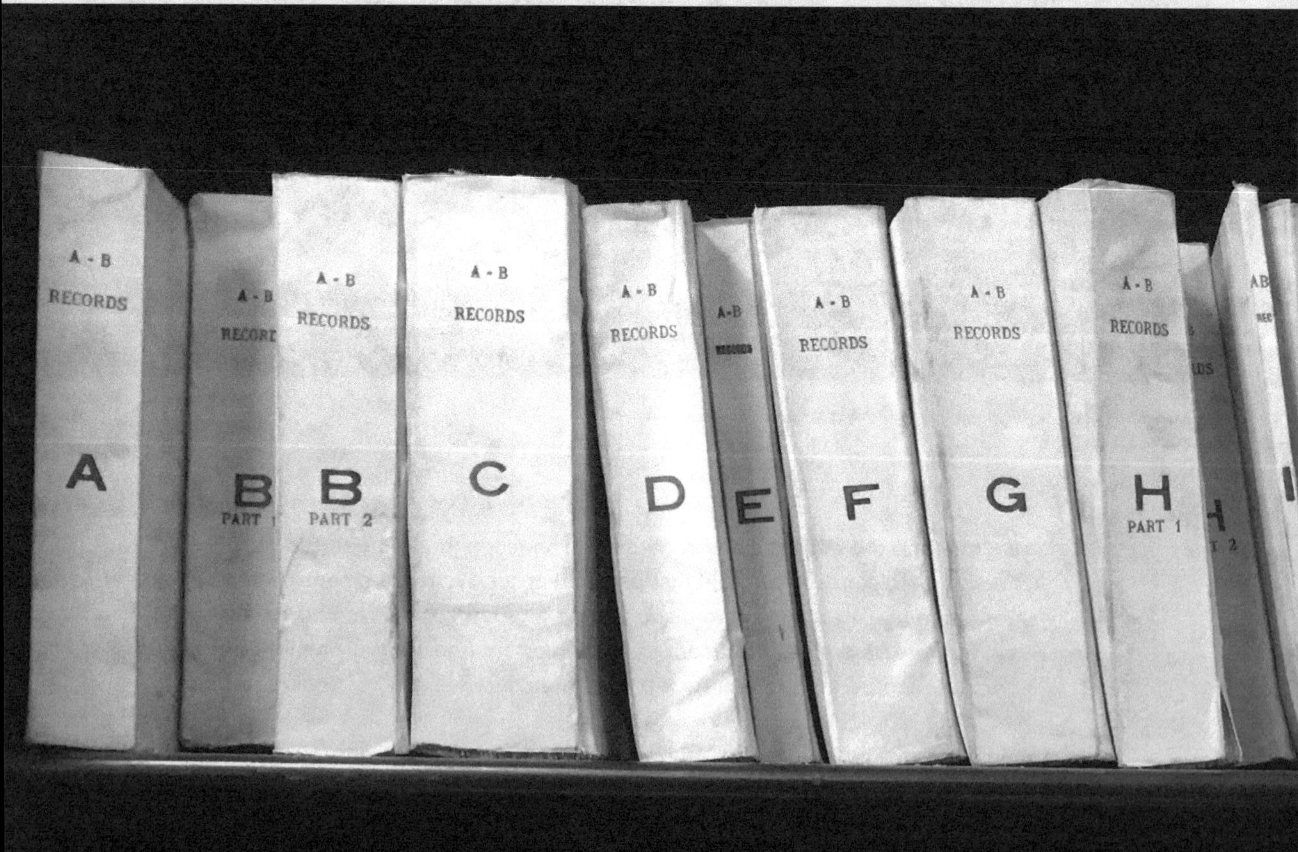

of the cabinets of dust and debris, including garbage tossed onto them many years ago. We have removed the ancient lunches and the emptied the gin bottles we found and cleaned up the remnants of a pigeon's nest.[4]

To arrive at that final state, we sometimes must work through dirt, and plenty of it. Because there is dirt, we need to remember the practical—because we are practical people. We need to ensure we protect ourselves and those we work with from the dirt. For this reason, we have jumpsuits to keep our clothes clean,[5] respirators to clean the air we breathe, goggles to protect our eyes, and even gloves to protect our hands. Because we need to be healthy to create a healthy archives.

But maybe I don't wear my gloves all the time.

ASSIGNMENT BUREAU RECORDS INDEX VOLUMES (1860–1929)

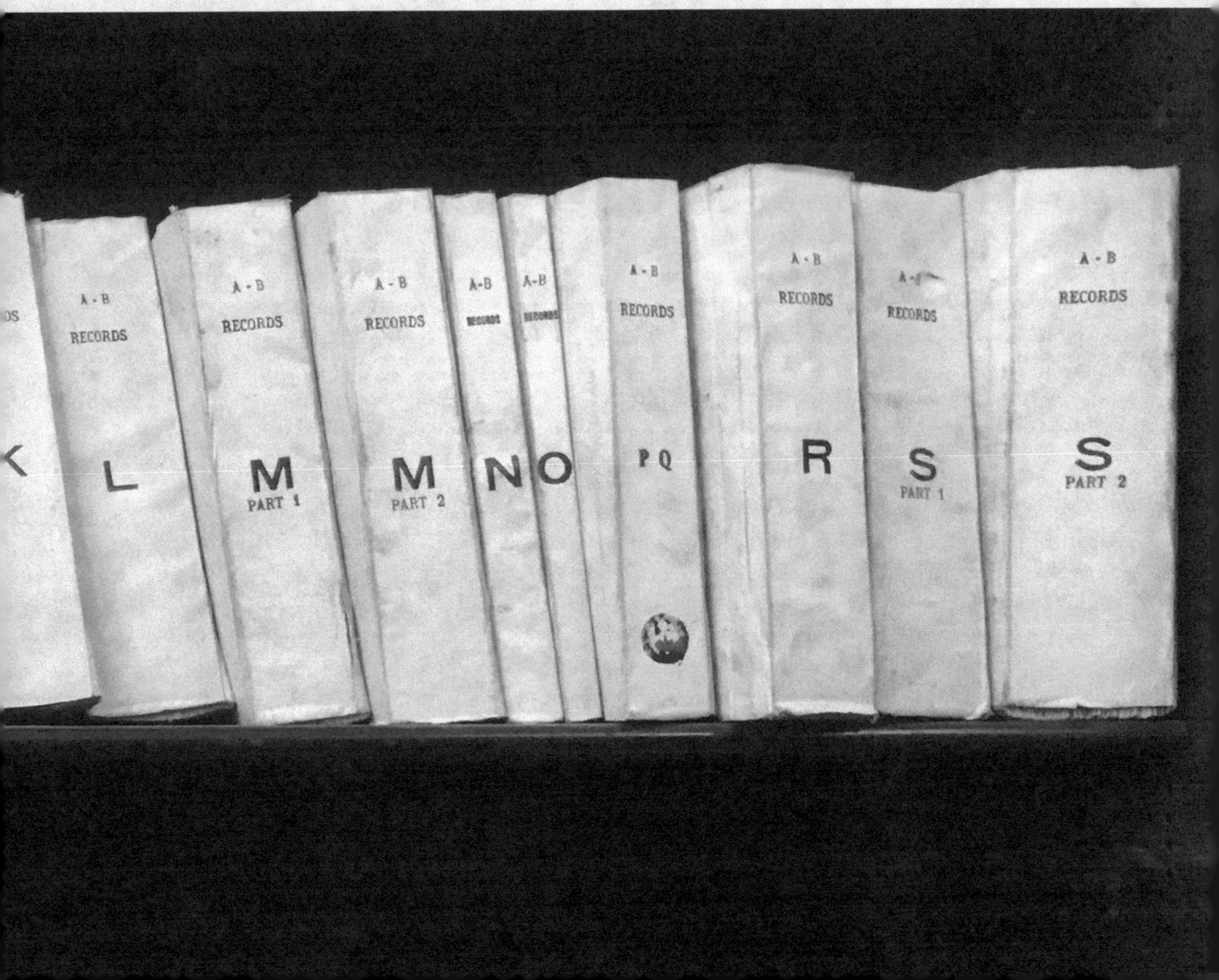

We must be prepared to abandon the concept of archives as bodies of "historical" records over against so-called active records which are put to sleep during their dormant years prior to salvation or extinction.

Hugh A. Taylor, "Information Ecology and the Archives of the 1980s," in "Imagining Archives: Essays and Reflections," ed. Terry Cook and Gordon Dodds (Rowan & Littlefield: Lanham, 2003): 96.

#archivesquotes

Interpretation of Record

The world of archives abounds with terminology consisting of self-confirming contradictions. For instance, a core term for archivists is the word *document*, which as a noun refers to a physically separate record often within a set of records. But as a verb, it refers to the purpose of that record itself: to document (record) an act. Additionally, archivists use *document* to refer to their own work. They might, for instance, acquire a set of records to document (provide evidence of) a particular human activity they determine is important enough to remember.

Archivists employ the word *record* in a similar way. As a noun, a record could be a certain line in a ledger book, the entire ledger book itself, or even (usually preceded by *a* rather than *the*) a set of ledger books serving as a complete accounting of that activity. Yet as a verb (but with a different pronunciation) the ledger books themselves record that activity.

Often, words carry more than one meaning, or shades of the same meaning, making them polysemous, and thus at least partially contradictory in meaning. Interpreting language is a complex task that takes us a lifetime to master.

Imagine, then, that you have come upon a record, say a small book, handwritten and carrying little information to identify its origins—which archivists might call its provenance, but we use that word (with a pronunciation contrary to the norm) to refer to something slightly different from a record's origin, though also that. Let us say the book does not announce what it is with a title, it does not include the name of an author (which would be the creator, in archivists' parlance), and it does not even carry any date.

Upon discovering this book and flipping through its pages, you might consider it a mystery, something orbiting outside the usual enveloping ellipse of context, something possibly comprehensible, but also likely something you cannot quite fathom. Yet this is not quite right. As I say, The record tells us what it is. If that is so, how do we understand this record?

By immersing ourselves within it, by reading the text long enough to unlock the secrets within it. We still might not understand all of it. Many records are not fully knowable, human communication changes with time, and we may not have adequate context to understand the record fully. But here is the fact: with or without supporting context, the record remains what it was upon its original completion. The record is not changed by the lack of context, which might consist of additional records created along with it, an understanding of the creators and systems that conceived of and produced the record, and even the particular uses of language common to the time of its creation.

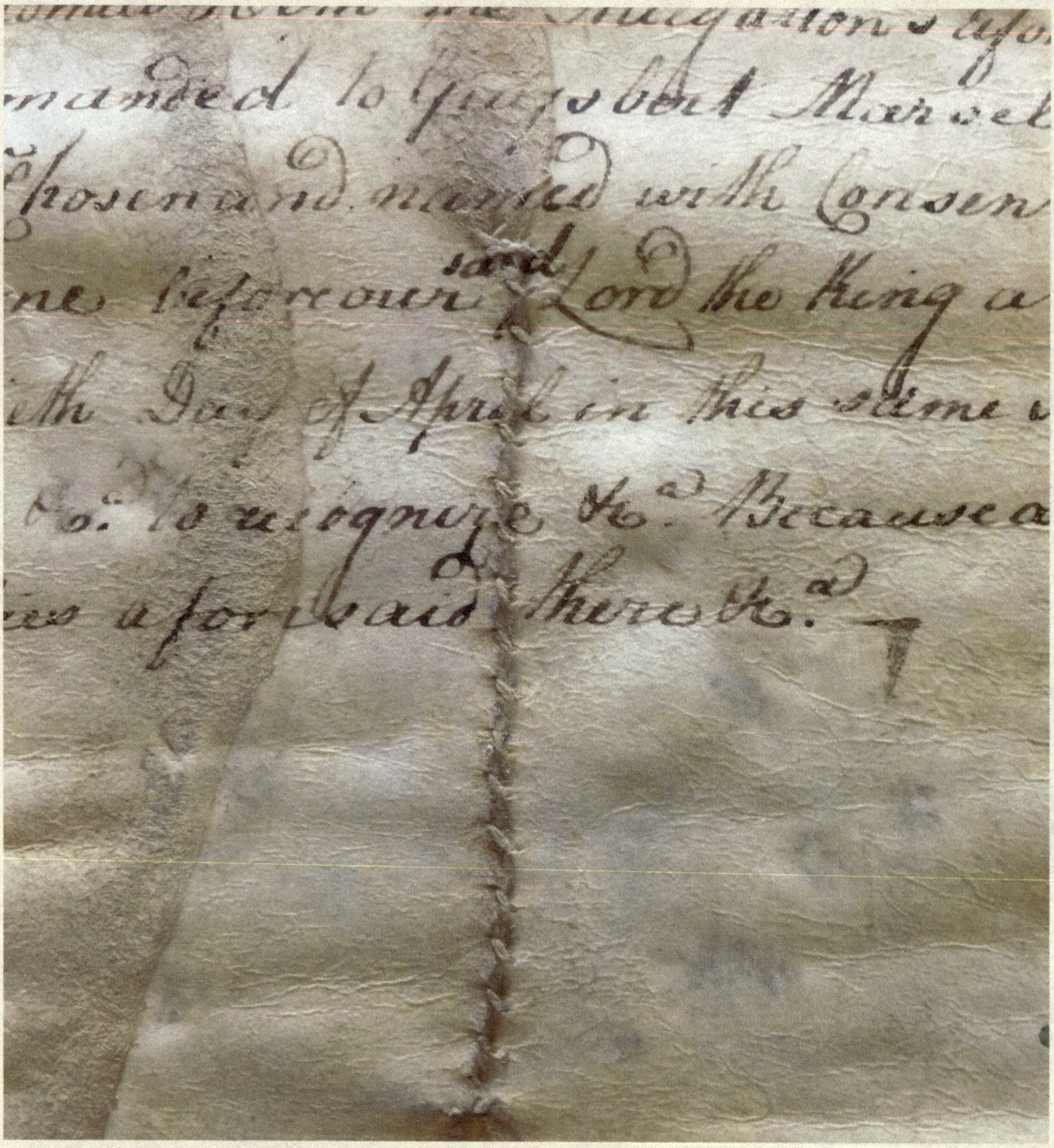

SUPREME COURT OF JUDICATURE CIVIL AND CRIMINAL PARCHMENTS (1684–1848), A PARCHMENT SUTURED SHUT

But the record is still wholly what it originally was.

This unavoidable fact sometimes befuddles us because we innately believe a record is what we understand about it, even though a record is merely the physical manifestation of a human action, not the interpretation of same. We can see the difference between the record and its interpretation with examples from languages we do not comprehend: A handwritten letter in Turkish seen by someone who does not read Turkish is still a letter in Turkish, written with certain instruments in a certain hand out of characters employed in that written language. If a modern Turk, who does not read the Arabic alphabet, finds an old letter in Turkish written with Arabic script, the person will not be able to read the letter, yet it will remain a letter in Turkish, one written in their native tongue.

Let us imagine that our record book is written in English, an English close enough in time to our current form of the language that we can understand it. Now, we can read the book, so we might believe we know it, and by reading it silently to ourselves we believe we know what it is. But knowing is not simple. It does not necessarily arise from the simple act of reading, even though it might.

Every message—oral, written, or signed; analog or digital; whole or fragmented—is encoded, so to understand it we must decode it. After reading for many years, we tend to believe decoding is easy because we can see a word on a page and immediately pronounce it into the air. But most writing is not a cipher, where one character merely replaces another and we can easily decipher the words with a simple key. Language is deep code. It is complex. Meaning can change merely by the context of the sentence, or the paragraph, or the times. Words appear before us in strings and their placement within a string may change their meaning.

We might believe we can see the pages of text before us, and maybe we can, but it is also possible that the handwriting in the text makes it difficult for us to decipher each letter correctly. Even if we succeed in transcribing the entire book into clear, readable, digital text, we may not fully understand the text.

This fact hovers over the reader as a quietly haunting ghost: The text is merely itself—messy or clean, clear or obfuscated—and the interpretation of the text (how we read and understand it) is always something different. Each of us reads any text from within the context of our own life, our own context of reading, our own experience of language, which means that our interpretations of any text will be different—though not necessarily by much—from that of anyone else.

We will understand one phrase slightly differently than most others will. The brief appearance of a single word of special significance to us personally will make us feel something others won't, will throw us back into a memory of an experience unreachable by others.

Every record is alone and simply itself, whether mundane or entrancing—and every reading of that record is a separate interpretation, a new experience never replicated outside each individual reader.

Extraordinary collections deserve a proper home, in all respects.

Karen Jamison Trivette, "Advocacy in Renovation Projects" (New England Archivists and Archivists Round Table of Metropolitan New York Joint Spring 2018 Meeting, New Haven, Connecticut, 23 March 2018).

#archivesquotes #NEAARTSP18

Archistory

I am not an historian, and I never wanted to be. This is an important fact to understand before I speak.

People with some idea of what archives are, including archivists themselves, sometimes tie archives to history a little too tightly. They state, baldy, that archives are the stuff from which history is written, which is almost and also partly true. History does not depend solely on records. Reminiscences, newspapers, artifacts, physical sites of human habitation, and even various secondary sources also serve to support the production of history. Archives are not sole source. The primacy archivists give to archives in this regard should not imply that archives are our only portals to the lost worlds of the past.

But archives are also not merely the handmaiden of history. Archives must represent the most abundantly valuable slivers of the universe of lived experience. They are always about the past, because the moment after we create a record it serves to remember that past. But the past is not merely the province of history as we usually imagine it: that field within the humanities focused on interpreting and contextualizing the activities of humans in the recorded past.

Archives must also preserve scientific data, and not simply for the stories about the people who created it or the advances they made possible—but also for the possible scientific reuse of those data. Archives sometimes must save data merely to allow us to administer the present, as well as understand the past. Archives must save records of how artists and writers worked, how philosophers fashioned their ideas, how humans molded the planet Earth into a thing never before imagined. Archives must be about all intellectual and social achievements and missteps of humanity. They must give us insight into how people fashioned their worlds—worlds otherwise lost to us. But the focus of archives as a broad human activity must be, instead, no focus at all. Instead, we need to create a view of every major segment of human activity, not merely one on history writ small.

To give a rough working definition of history, let me say that history is the remembered or recorded past. Certainly, we sometimes use the term to mean anything that happened in the past, whether stored as data or held in a body as memory. But history is generally regarded as that part of the past we can remember be-

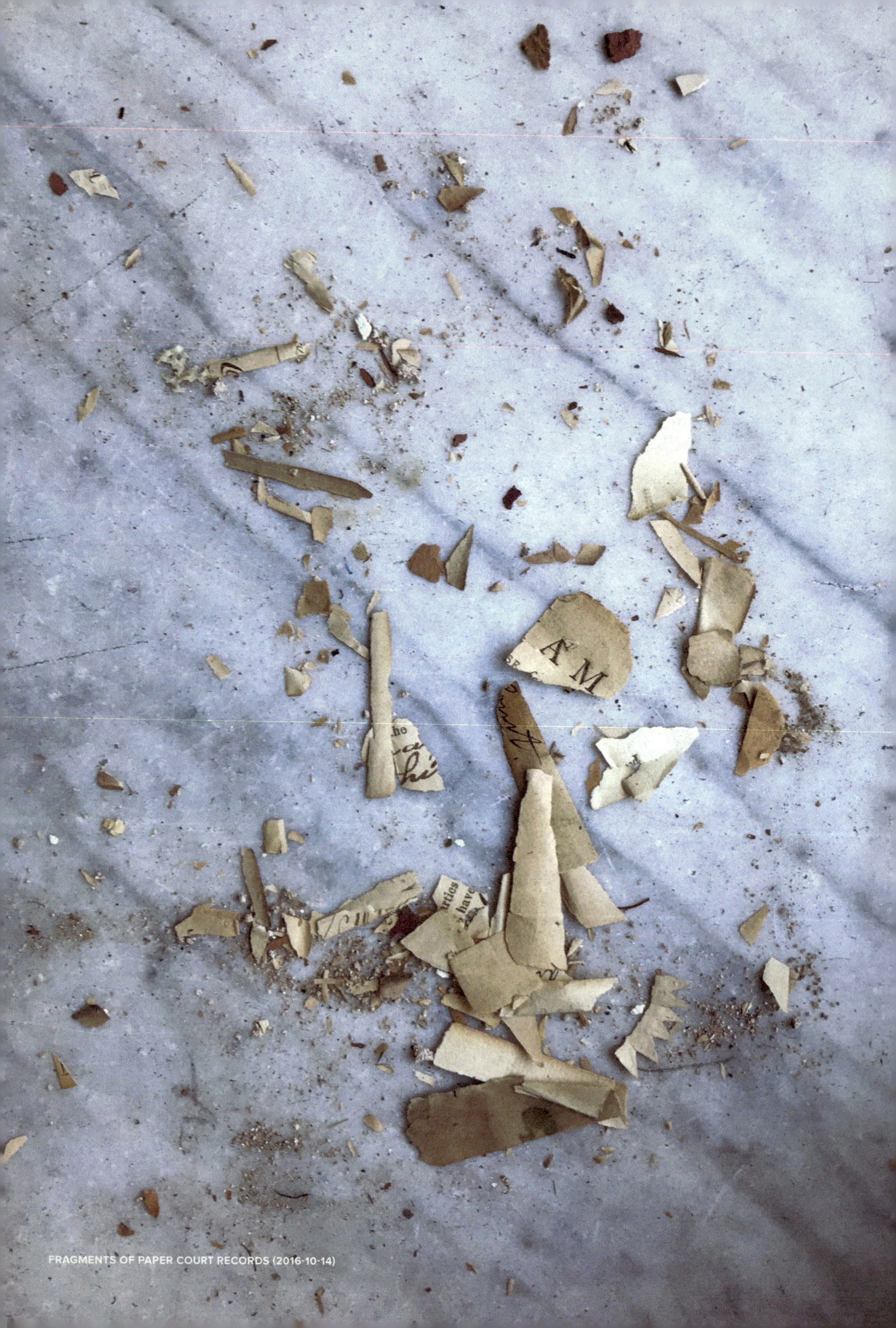

FRAGMENTS OF PAPER COURT RECORDS (2016-10-14)

cause it resides within our minds or is recorded in some way and thus interpreted into a story about the past, though not perfectly of the past. History is not a pure thing: it is not a movie reel of the past moving second by second through the meandering stream of one story now palpably gone from us. History is how we see the past now or have seen the past in a time now also past. In this way, it is distinctly different from archives.

Archives are something else, something solid, something we hope will be immutable. They are records saved for their continuing value to humanity—maybe not all of humanity in every case, but important for some significant segment of the billions of us who call this only place, this single planet, home. They are the evidence of the past, proof the past occurred, and an imperfect explanation of how it happened. Archives are stabilized data.

The difference between evidence in the form of data and history as a reconstruction of the past is huge. An archival record is always and permanently itself. We may each interpret or understand the data differently, yet the data do not change. History is that interpretation, not the original data. History is constructed from a certain vantage point and based on assumptions both knowable and unknowable by its maker. The data in archives are created organically to support a human activity—at least to a degree greater than this is true for history. Archives are, we might say, composed of organic data, where the data of history is inorganic.

History is an amalgam of data, assumptions about the data and about their lacunae, and a reconstitution of the data to create a story out of the past. And the past is not made of clean sequential stories. It consists of human and other activities that have already occurred yet lack a clear sequence for each of its events. The edges of a story are not known. One person may include one episode of that inchoate story, yet another may leave it out, identifying it as superfluous—maybe believing it part of another story we do not yet know.

Of course, this boundary between archives and history is not clear and clean. The archives of an historian's attempt to write accurate history will show the story of that process, so those records will be authentic documentation—we should hope—of the sculpting of that history, even though the story itself is strained through the mind of the historian. Archives may be the organic detritus of acts of reliable creation, yet biases will still arise within their data. Even machine-generated data are driven by the influencing biases of the people writing the code that collects them.

This slender difference between these interrelated human activities is important to me, because the goal of the archivist is the management of data, not the writing or even the telling of history. *Data* is a difficult term for some archivists to embrace because it appears to have a cold clinical feel to it. History carries, ever within itself, as a word, the concept of story, so it seems to be the manifestation of the human urge to tell a tale that will move another.

But data is our province. I became an archivist not because I wanted to be an historian but because data, in all its multitudinous forms, entrances me. We are the only creatures who preserve our thoughts or record our movements. Data is evidence of the human, and it always is, even when the human per se is not its focus. Data is how we remember before our lifetimes began and how others remember us after those lifetimes end.

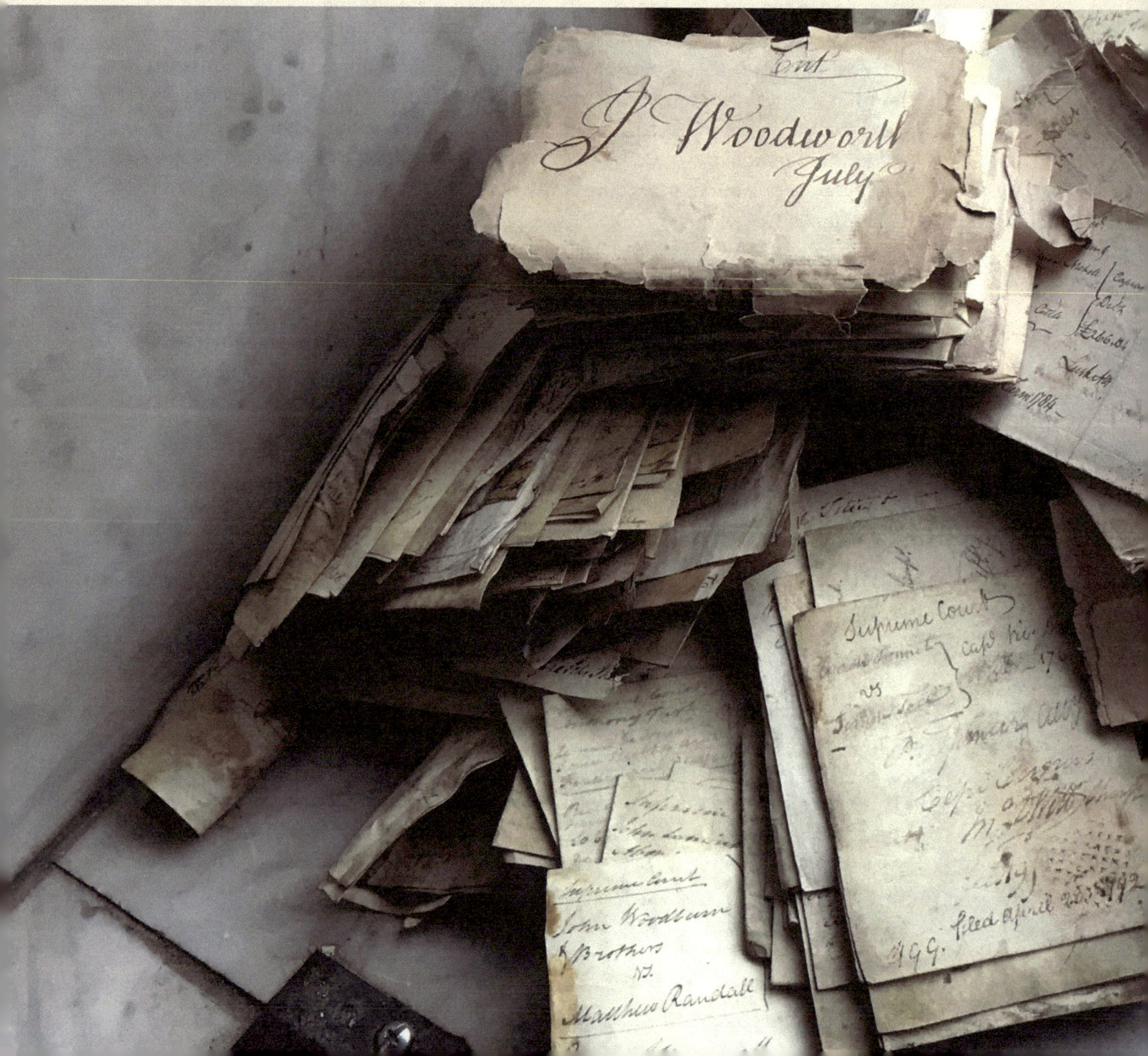

If we pretend to be historians, or even if we believe that the work of archives is history, we abandon the richness of human experience. We cut off most of the world to look backwards through a spyglass at the ever-diminishing past. We become blind to the horizon, to the curvature of the earth, to the movements of the planets, because all we see is one speck of humanity, rich and vital, but now far away, because we have torn it out of the whole, because we have isolated it.

Because we have decided to love the fragment detached from the organic and universal whole.

UNORGANIZED PARCHMENT WRITS OF THE SUPREME COURT OF JUDICATURE

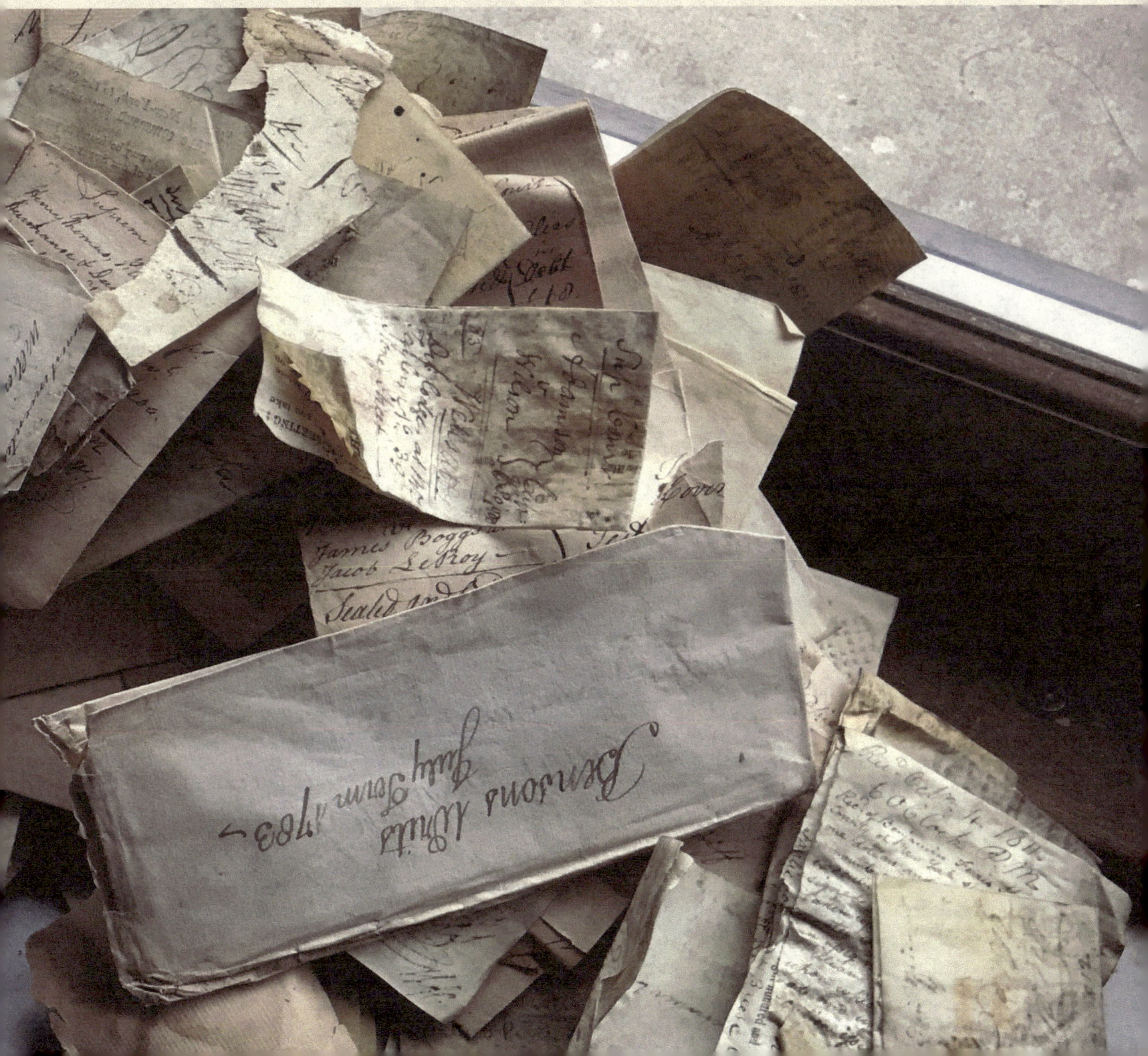

Because it's not about records. It's about people.

David Carmicheal, "Between a Rock and a Hard Place: Archivists at the Confluence of Past and Future," Plenary (Mid-Atlantic Regional Archives Conference: Pittsburgh, 15 April 2016).

#archivesquotes

Remembering the Future: The Core Relevance of Archives

Forget the past. Focus on knowledge.[1]

That is my advice to archivists, of which I am one.[2] It is not that I denigrate the past or have no interest in it. The past is essential to the present. In fact, it created the present. In doing so, it has made itself invaluable to our present, which itself disappears into the past in less than a moment.

The value of the past is clear. It allows us to understand our current situation—to put it in context, as an archivist might say. This occurs through the processes of remembered memory and recorded memory, and the connection to the past that archivists believe derives from the fact that recorded memory consists of records of various types. Even a book or an artifact are records in this amorphous use of the term, but most valuable of all among these recordings are archives, for they are unique (or nearly so) and they provide insights that may not be fully discoverable in the published world.

I do not complain about the past here. What I do say is that the past is the object of our profession but knowledge is its subject. We focus on the past, because the materials we appraise, manage, and provide access to come to us from the past and document that past. This fact sometimes causes us to believe our subject is history, but that is not the case. Our subject, our goal, our reason for being is knowledge—its collection, protection, dissemination, and creation.

When we lose sight of that, we lose sight of the power of archives and of archivists.

The source of archives' power comes primarily from the information they record. Archives have other sources of power over human consciousness (the emotional power of inherent value, the ideational power of historical significance, even the potential financial power of monetary value), but it is archives' power to answer questions, solve problems, and create knowledge that are key. It is not enough for us to enjoy old stuff—even though the sometimes stark difference between the old and our current new is part of what draws us to the record. We need to embrace the idea that knowledge is our goal.

A focus on knowledge also requires a focus on the future, because focusing on knowledge is never only about ideas from the past. It concerns the process of taking past knowledge and synthesizing it with knowledge from other current and past sources to develop new knowledge—to expand human understanding, potential, and accomplishment. We are drawn to archives maybe because of data (small bits of information that don't quite form a cohesive thought), we remain in archives because we see how these data become stores of rich information, and we succeed in archives when we make the most of this information (often through the intervention of others, the users of the records) to create new knowledge.

I say this not to suggest that archivists are not knowledge makers. We are. Our making is merely of a different character. Our role is to create systems to keep that knowledge intelligible and to ensure the accurate interpretation of archives. Systems of archival knowledge consist of two elements: the selection of records and the creation and maintenance of archival contextualization.

Selection, of course, is the process of appraisal—a process I believe is more often honored by the tongue than the hand. Too much appraisal consists of decisions foisted on archivists, swiftly rendered intuitive conclusions, or the rote following of past practice. Appraisal, our most essential act and the initial process in producing archives, determines everything important about an archives: what it will keep—and why. The fundamental purpose of archives is to assemble bodies of records that make sense together and that increase in value by being brought together. Many archivists deride the concept of "collection,"[3] because it suggests to them artificiality, rather than something organic and naturally structured—but I say archives are always artificial, to a degree. They are created, whether by wit or whim, out of organic wholes, yet they almost never consist of the entire organized structure of the original information environment. An archive is a précis of a set of records, not the entirety of it. We must blow away the chaff to see and collect the grain. We cannot save the whole world, so we save that part of it we assess as essential.

The process of appraisal usually encompasses multiple fonds or subfonds, so we are always creating a collection of records, even if that collection consists of records from the same central fonds. In a manuscripts environment, this is even more so the case, yet the collection we create out of various manuscripts collections functions best when the records have conceptual connections between them. For this reason, manuscript repositories usually collect in certain areas, thus producing a somewhat artificial supracollection of records, but of records that relate to one another because of subject focus or the relationship of the creators to each other. In creating such collections, we enhance the value of the records because the individual manuscript groups become more than the sum of their discrete parts when they fit, exist, and are contextualized together.

In my thinking, the second critical knowledge-making activity of archivists is archival contextualization, which is the most important part of processing. If we define processing in the traditional way (arrangement plus description and maybe including rehousing), contextualization is part of description but in ways that may reach beyond the realm of one fonds, that incorporate related records into an archival system that envelops records from various sources into the same cocoon of meaning. In my purely archival work, I focus on a suprafonds encompassing the records of a couple of dozen courts operating from 1674 until (in some cases) today. My primary activity with these records is to build a sturdy enough contextual structure to make these records knowable to the future.

This archival contextualization is my most important work. My small unit carries out many activities with these records: we HEPA-vacuum them, we box them, we label the boxes, we describe the records, we record their locations. We bring order (or instill order) to records that have sometimes lain unattended for decades. We help make the records more usable. But my true focus is on making the re-

HE FURTHER S (FOUND VISUAL POEM BY GEOF HUTH, 2016-12-06)

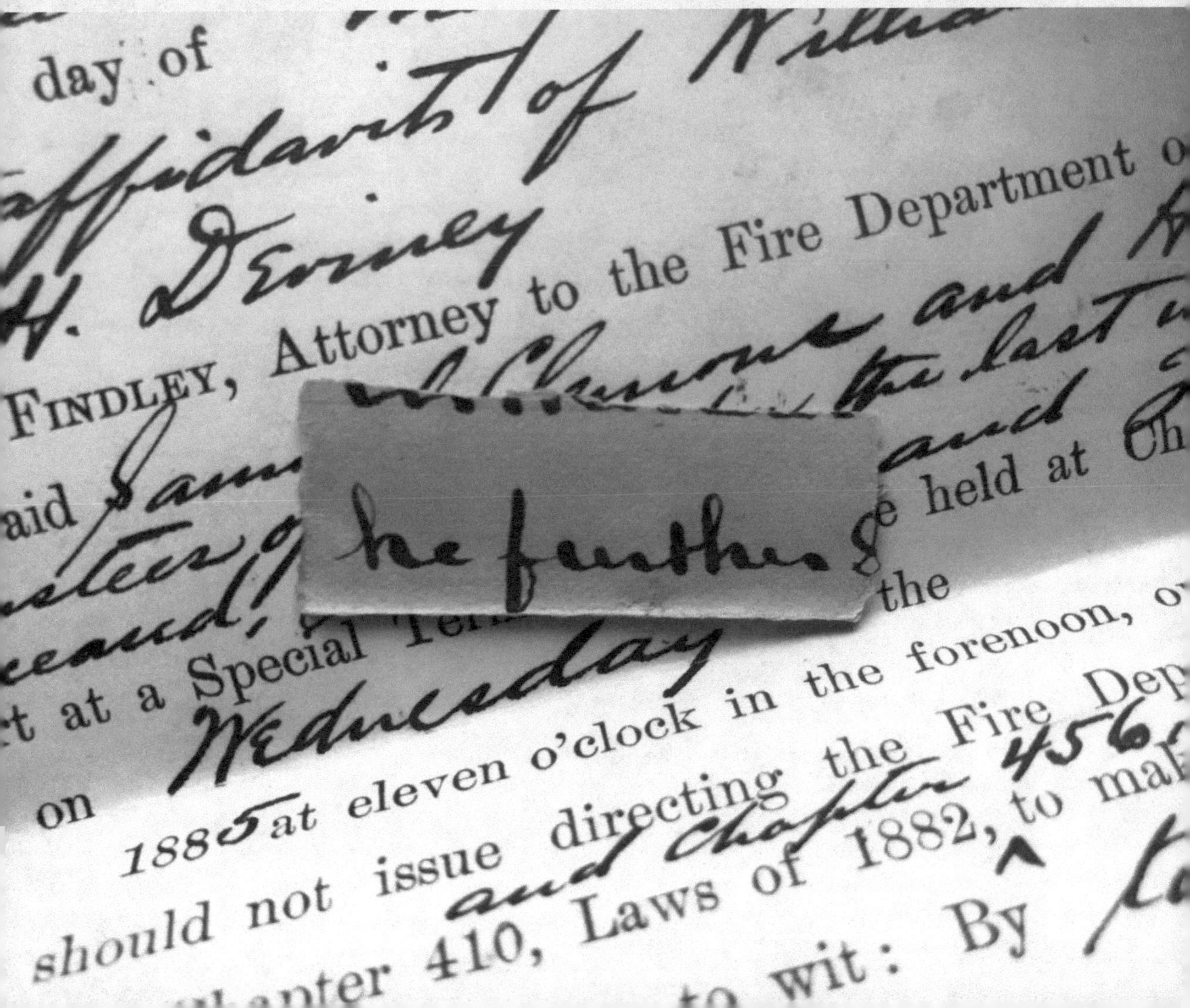

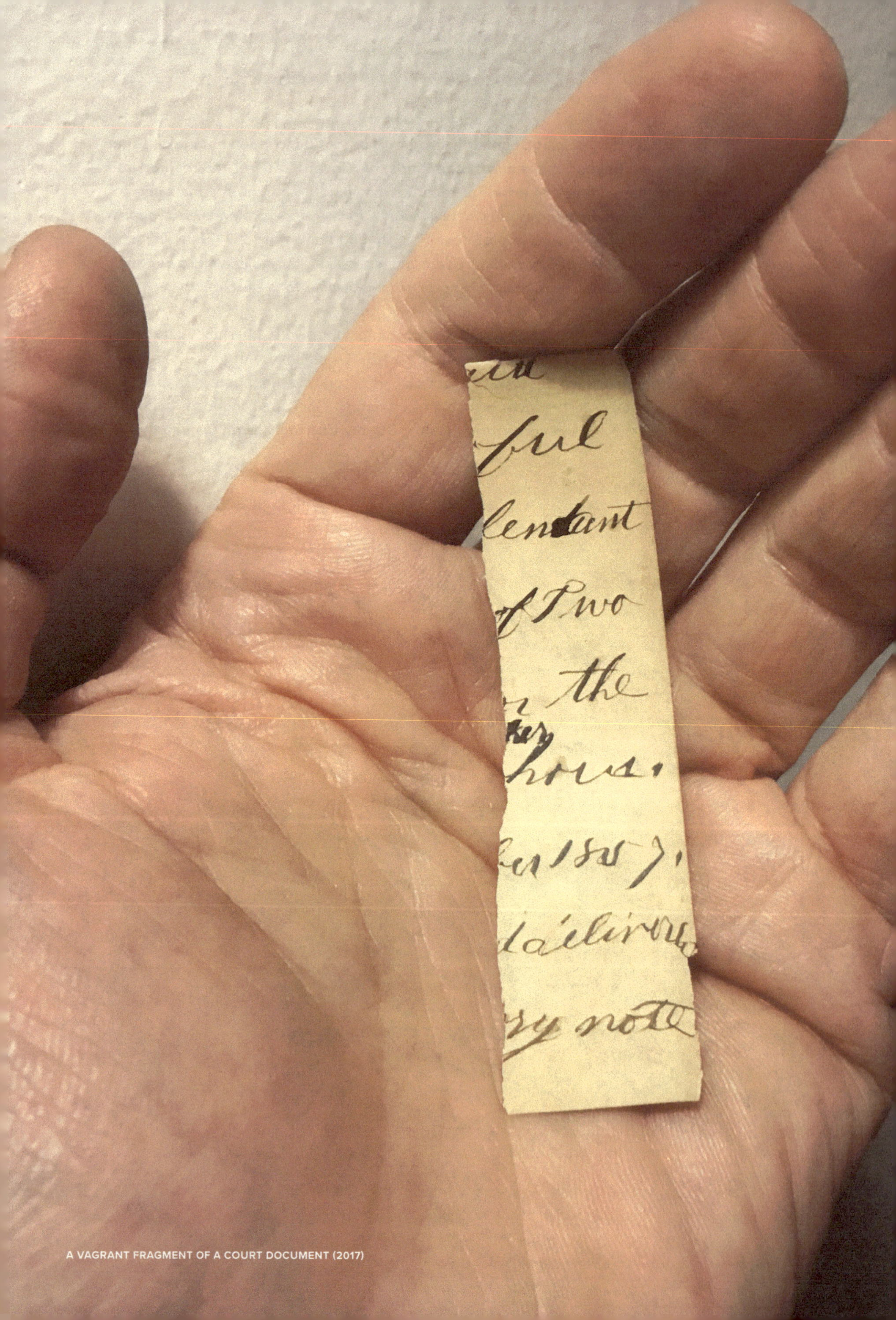

A VAGRANT FRAGMENT OF A COURT DOCUMENT (2017)

cords knowable. I do this[4] by trying to grasp the entirety of the records hoard, by developing personal knowledge of all the courts, all the series, all the processes that made these records. The necessary next step is to record the knowledge I have collected or created—whether that information came from the records themselves, from the work of previous custodians, or from outside sources (such as, commonly in my case, the chapter laws of New York).

And determining how to present contextualizing knowledge is my most difficult job, and the one I am least sure I complete successfully. The easy part is dealing with contextualization at the series level. All the metadata we assemble to make a series understandable: the series title (often created by the archivist), the date range (sometimes a mystery to the creator), and the series description. It is in the last that archival contextualization takes its honored place. By describing what we've learned about the records (and also about the creator and its processes), we provide some basic context for understanding the records. This may seem superfluous sometimes, when records seem perfectly clear in their purpose and intent, but many records are opaque to users even if transparent to archivists. And I—standing in for the archivist at the moment—discover almost every week records that are a total mystery to me, until I take the time to allow the records to tell me what they are. Our job is to remove the process of deciphering the general meaning and purpose of the records so the user can focus on understanding what the record might valuably reveal.

I like replacing the term "finding aid" with "knowing aid." The finding aid focuses on allowing users to find records, a valuable goal but one lacking in depth of purpose. The knowing aid helps people interpret the records accurately, understand them in their natural and extranatural[5] contexts, and know the records. Knowing is key. Records can be cryptic, inscrutable, unknowable. Our job is to create as much of a contextual superstructure as the user will need to make sense of the record. This might mean explaining the processes and reasons why organizations or individuals created records, how interconnected organizations (such as various courts in a system of courts) fit and operated together, or how the archivist determined that records found physically remote from each still formed a single series.

The possible types of context an archivist could document are practically infinite, so we need to determine what context is the most essential—which sometimes might be the context most likely to slip out of the realm of human knowledge. Since our project is knowledge, the creation, maintenance, and expansion of knowledge remains our primary goal. We should remember this, and remember that we do this for the future, which is the only world left for us to enlighten.

No collective memory is complete without a countermemory.

Jeannette A. Bastian, "Flowers for Homestead: A Case Study in Archives and Collective Memory," *The American Archivist* 72:1 (Spring/Summer 2009): 126.

#archivesquotes

Stuff and Non-Stuff

Archivists, usually a technical breed of person, often use the word *stuff* to refer to their holdings. Their use of this term is, to some degree, precise. To talk (and even write) about *stuff* is to use one word to encompass all the records an archivist or archivists oversee by using but a single, likely Germanic, word of ignoble birth. *Stuff* is a word that has multiplied the number of its meanings over the centuries while simultaneously diluting its core sense. The *Oxford English Dictionary*'s attempt to corral the most diaphanous sense of *stuff* is this wonderful phrase:

Matter of an unspecified kind.[1]

And so it is. This is the sense archivists employ, with a little extra meaning slipped in for our purposes. Our matter of an unspecified kind is usually the archival materials[2] we have professional responsibility for. Stuff—as a word, rather than a physical reality—is easy; it is simple; it cannot be inaccurate because its game is not accuracy but generality. It serves as our word of choice for collections as a mass. In a world void of cohesive fonds or burdened with them, stuff is the glue that binds disparate creators' works into one set: the supracollection overseen by most archivists. That collection of collections that is our own small but rich homeland.

What the word *stuff* does for us is aggregate disaggregations. As archivists, we believe in a bond between records[3] that shows us they are of one piece. But when we think that way, we are imagining the fonds of an entire organization or one encompassing the life of a single individual. We are imagining records with natural connective tissue holding them together. But this assumes one sense of the word *archives*, while we live in a world where that word contains many senses.[4]

In a university archives and special collections, we are likely to find the university's archives themselves, thematic collections of collections (such as the Death Penalty Archive at the University at Albany, SUNY), and disparate manuscript collections and organizational fonds collected by the institution. Some of these categories of records will have true archival connective tissue, others will share a focus but have no organic connection to other sets of records, and some of these collections will have not a hint of a link to any of the other sets of records.

Yet something holds them together. Though disparate and disconnected intellectually and corporally, these records are connected by the repository that holds them. The records of the world make sense within their particular contexts, which I claim are myriad and plentiful, never singular.[5] A record changes even when its locational context changes. At the granular level, if a single document is separated physically from its brethren, it loses its physical context, making it more difficult for us to understand it properly. In our larger idea of context here, the record gains meaning by being associated with records it is not organically connected to. The record becomes part of a larger body of records, one assembled by archivists, and this tells us something about the records as it also tells us something about the archivist and the archives itself. The acquisition policy of the organization will (or should—you never can tell with such things) tell us why these records were valuable enough to accession. We understand their value in the context of the process of their collection.

And that newly acquired collection becomes part of the *stuff* of that archives. It has returned to the home it never had before, and it is now a transplanted native, honored by the umbrella term *stuff*. Which returns us to the stuff of archives.

We usually use the term *stuff* in a neutral way. English devised the word to give us an easy way to discuss general aggregations of things, including actions, so it is all purpose and thus heavily used by archivists. Take a look at these uses I've found of the term:

> Several years ago at a meeting of the Society of Georgia Archivists, Margaret Child of the National Endowment for the Humanities exclaimed, "There's just too much stuff." The "stuff" she was referring to is primarily the records of modern times which are making their way into archives and local repositories. Child believes that her cry and that of the modern records archivist "will soon become desperate." (Kathy Roe Coker)[6]

> Who will do this, however? Unquestionably, we need to partner with information technology staff in our institutions. It seems less likely, however, that they will do all the heavy lifting for us. It's our mandate, they reason, not their's [*sic*]. Nor will it likely suffice to simply have a resident wizard, that computer geek we hide in the closet until we need something done with this stuff. (Leon J. Stout)[7]

The archivist asks how much material and what sort of formats were included in the collection, but the donor rambles on about the scholarly richness of his papers. Finally, she [the archivist] blurts out the question: “How much stuff do you have?” Following a few moments of silence, the offended potential donor responds by saying that what he had “was not ‘stuff,’ but history.” Archivists and donors frequently refer to the abstract and unseen archival and manuscript materials as “stuff,” but in this situation the archivist apologized and better articulated the question. (Aaron D. Purcell)[8]

As an archivist who works with personal digital archives, the notion that managing our digital stuff can be reduced to a science is certainly an appealing one. (Dorothy Waugh)[9]

Besides indicating generalness, the term also appears to refer to volume. As a matter of fact, I have yet to find any similar use of the term in the archives literature predating the 1980s, by which point volume was already a pressing issue for archivists. The term has a homey connotation to it, suggesting something that we are well familiar with, something that surrounds us and provides shelter from the elements, but we also employ the term in a deprecated sense, though otherwise carrying the same meaning:

Left to the marketplace, archives become like history textbook writers trying to fit in everything and doing it on an equal playing field; the “textbooks fall apart” or do not get written at all, and the archives become repositories of lots of interesting stuff without real coherence or focus. (Richard J. Cox)[10]

Most, if not all, archival repositories hold collections and major series within collections that staff members do not want and would never consider accepting now. This is the “stuff” that causes archivists to shake their heads and ask: “What were we thinking when we took this in?” (Mark A. Greene)[11]

> We need to make sure our archival institutions are platforms for meaning-making. Everyone in this room knows that archives are more than just storehouses of old stuff. Archives are sites of learning, identity-building, and personal growth. (Kate Theimer)[12]

These uses of the term illuminate the negative elements of stuff—although Theimer uses the derogatory sense only to swat it away. And it seems appropriate that Cox and Greene—two great archival intellects but also prickly personalities[13]—would use the term in this clear-eyed and practical sense. They know our archives contain detritus anyone can live without and that some archives' acquisition policies are either vague and unhelpful or imperfectly followed, leading to supracollections with indiscernable guiding principles. A beacon that never hits a solid surface illuminates only itself.

As we might say, stuff abides. We hold onto this word, and we use it to encapsulate our entire universe. Stuff *is* archives.

In searching for relevant quotations, here and there, I ran across one that appears to guide me toward my unexpected yet predetermined conclusion to this brief essay, and it seems quite appropriate that these words come from Terry Cook, one of the most successful thinkers and doers in our profession[14]:

> From researchers' perspective, the issue is clear: they want the stuff, and care not whether it comes from the Library reference room on the second floor or the Archives reference room on the third floor in the Wellington Street building, or from one or two Websites. (Terry Cook)[15]

For, you see, stuff can include non-stuff, just as archives—or the superabundant repositories we call special collections—hold not just records, but books, ephemera, even artworks and artifacts. I make a clear distinction between stuff (archives) and non-stuff (everything else), but that doesn't mean the line between the two is clear or that there is greater value in purity of effort. Or that users care if the information they need is available as a record, a book, or an object.

Almost anything physical or digital can be a record, at least in some sense. My personal papers, to give an example easily at hand, include documentation in almost every format conceivable: paper, audio tape (cassette and reel), videotape, 16mm film, printed photographs, and various formats of digital media and digital files—documents, photographs, videos, databases (for I am a data person), etc. All these feel like archives to us. They certainly could be records.

But there is other recordlike stuff or non-stuff among my papers. There are books of two types: copies of books I've written (almost entirely poetry) and books I've owned and heavily annotated—the marginalia within them allowing me to see these as records.[16] This collection includes thousands of poems of many types, hundreds and hundreds of which are objects—sometimes constructed objects, but usually found objects that I've filled or covered with words and images, ink and paint. Others might consider these nothing more than sculptures—a statement made more believable because some of these are now on exhibit.[17] I consider each one of these a record as much as I consider the final copy of a poem on paper or the copy of a poem printed in a book as a record. Why would I not? Beyond these types of non-stuff, the papers include a painted portrait of me, which we might not think of as a record—but which we would naturally see as a record if it were a print of a photograph, or even the digital file of same. A record is documentation of something that happened—not just of a transaction, but also of an act of creation itself.

I believe archives must focus on the record itself—whatever that might mean—but we also must accept that we sometimes become the inheritors or acquirers of objects that have at least some enduring significance. Sometimes—let's take the example of the thousands of ceremonial shovels stored in archives around the country—this significance is small or questionable. At other times, artifacts have deep cultural and emotive significance. Objects from a person's life or documenting the history of an organization contain data just as much as records do. The information is merely encoded differently, and the means of understanding objects differs a bit.

Yet all of these are objects. A record in paper or digital form is still an object. (We even call the latter digital objects.) Sometimes, to document a life or organization, we need a broader array of object types—we need to include some that are more objectual.[18] Our acquisition policies should never focus on such non-stuff, but they should allow for the collection of them when necessary, because sometimes the most robust archives are those that hold records and books and artifacts—those that include the cultural or intellectual record in the broadest sense of the word.

For these reasons, I cherish stuff and non-stuff alike.

A personal moral compass is necessary for a meaningful archival purpose.

Scott Cline, “Beyond Measure: Telling the Story of Archival Value” (Society of American Archivists Conference, Atlanta, Georgia, 5 August 2016).

#archivesquotes

Document the Network

In manuscript collections, archivists often focus on the individual. With pure archives, the focus is on the parent organization. These tendencies belie an interest in the great writer or artist, in the important institution, one that sometimes allows us lose sight of the importance of documenting networks of activity, instead of their nodes.

I, as a human being, am a human node in many networks: familial, professional, personal, literary, artistic. Probably because of this, I believe information exists in a universe of dense and intertwining contexts. A record, for instance, from the New York Mayor's Court in 1674 connects to all the court's successors but also to the Dutch court that preceded it (and by which its own name and form were significantly influenced) and to the courts its work overlapped with contemporaneously. Information has no clear border. Information from one node of a network connects (often invisibly, conceptually) to other nodes in other networks. Just as a leaf drops off a tree and decays into the forest floor creating soil and a maple key is blown miles to lodge itself in good enough soil to grow a new tree, information is being passed among networks in almost random ways as the work of various nodes operate with others points in the network, all of them sharing information and feeding off the other.

Instead of thinking of these networks as information networks, I like to conceptualize them as neural networks. Data or a single datum may exist at one point in the network, but it can be transferred to another point—even unconsciously—to accumulate data into information, something that can transfer an idea, a significant enough set of recorded facts to allow us to understand what we are seeing. Data is transferred—formally and informally, in recorded and spoken form—across a single network and across all the networks it intersects with. We usually think of information networks as systems of recorded information, because those are the systems that can persist over time. But networks are also oral. Information is passed along by voices in person or through telephone lines and data networks. These voices are rarely saved (except occasionally in the deprecated form of voicemails), but they still form part of the network, just an evanescent part.

All the archivist sees is what remains in the end (or was selected by the archivist for retention), which is never the whole network, because the entire network is too large to control, too much to store. So we pick the nodes to collect: the papers of a famous novelist, but maybe not those of another novelist, relatively unknown, who was a close friend and influencer of the first; the records of a group in our state opposing capital punishment, but maybe not the papers of a closely aligned group in a far-off state. The nodes are valuable, but we cannot care for all of recorded humanity, so we must choose.

We must, however, appraise and collect and consider records in the bewilderingly complex context of their native networks, obvious and obscure, near at hand and far-flung. And we must consider the possibility that it is not the node itself that should be our focus, but the network in which the nodes operate. We need to believe that the famous flagbearers of causes or organizations may not be as important as the causes and organizations themselves. Instead of believing in the primacy of the person, we need to believe in the value of humanity. To put this idea in context, answer this question: What does a mass of information show us that a focused point of fact cannot?

To illustrate this concept, which certainly draws on thinking about documentation strategy and how it can fill gaps in archives—in the kept human record—let me use myself as an example.

A few weeks ago, I had a conversation with a scholar about his work on Robert Grenier, a fine and radical minimalist poet, whose most famous published works are often hard to find, and who has influenced my minimalist poetry, even though I practiced that form of writing radically myself for decades before I realized his existence. During our discussion, the scholar noted that poets often said to him that they wished someone would write a book about their poetry, meaning (essentially) a book about themselves. The scholar noted that only a small number of Ph.D. students receive degrees in English-language literature each year, and that only a small percentage of those will focus on poetry—and a smaller number yet on contemporary poetry—yet hundreds of poets are self-created a year. Thus, there is no way there will ever be enough scholars available even to focus on all of the most important poets of their time.

Being a poet, I know well only one thing about us: we speak falsely all the time. When we discuss poetry, we exaggerate its importance, we try to heighten its value, based usually on just a few poems or a few poets who have spoken so powerfully to us that we hear their words reverberating in our ears and feel a tingling slipping down our spine. Also, the myth of the poet as some brave individual struggling an entire life to speak truth into a truthless world allows us to overemphasize our importance. (To be sure, the opposites of these points are also true. Poets are usually the most severe critics of poetry in general. We know how to highlight the valuelessness of our own work.)

So I responded to the scholar with something like this: What are they even thinking? The poet is not the important one. The poet is merely a representative of a set of poets. The poet is part of a network, and what we need to document is the network: the movement, not the individual.

Here's how I have considered this issue with my own personal papers. Before my papers were taken in by an archives (at their request, not my suggestion), I considered where to put them, and I had three places in mind: The Avant-Writing Collection at the Ohio State University, The Poetry Collection at the University at Buffalo, or the M.E. Grenander Department of Special Collections and Archives at the University at Albany. (Because of the recently announced transfer this year of the Ruth and Marvin Sacker Archive of Concrete and Visual Poetry to the University of Iowa, I might have considered Iowa a possibility as well.)

Among these repositories, my preferred repository was the University at Albany. Since I used to live near Albany, that propinquity was certainly an advantage, because I knew I would need occasional access to the papers—but that was not my major concern. What drove me to put my papers in Albany was to protect a node of my network, one I shared with many others. The other two repositories collected and held the papers of many people in my networks. They also collected the books and zines we produced. If I had donated my papers to one of those, my papers would have significantly overlapped with those of others. Every physical storage facility has a unique set of risks associated with it, and I didn't want an even larger body of records of my network's activity to be in risk of simultaneous destruction. Thus, I chose the repository that documented no other node of my network.

There is a counter-argument to mine: it will be easier for researchers if like records reside in the same space, and that is certainly true. For instance, to read my voluminous paper correspondence with my deceased friend Bob Grumman, you would have to travel to the Ohio State University in Columbus, but to read Bob's responses to me you would have to travel to Albany—and the drive takes an entire day. I don't argue against having collections of collections in a single reposition. Doing so is common because it has value: it makes use easier for researchers, it allows archivists to become expert in a certain field of collection, and it allows users and archivists both the opportunity to view a significant portion of a network and thus better understand the network.

But this doesn't undermine my point. Dispersal, even of incompletely duplicative material from a single network, helps to protect an outline of the network. The future is never made up out of the entire past. It always appears before us shadowy and a bit indistinct, but without dispersal—conjoined with heightened levels of specialization and focus—we can design systems of information-keeping that are too susceptible to disaster. We can turn the past, at least for selected slices of the recorded past, into lacunae.

Such an idea requires us to think collaboratively as collectors of records. Too often, we focus so much on our urge to create significant bodies of archives that we become blind to the dangers of saturated areas of collection. Through a

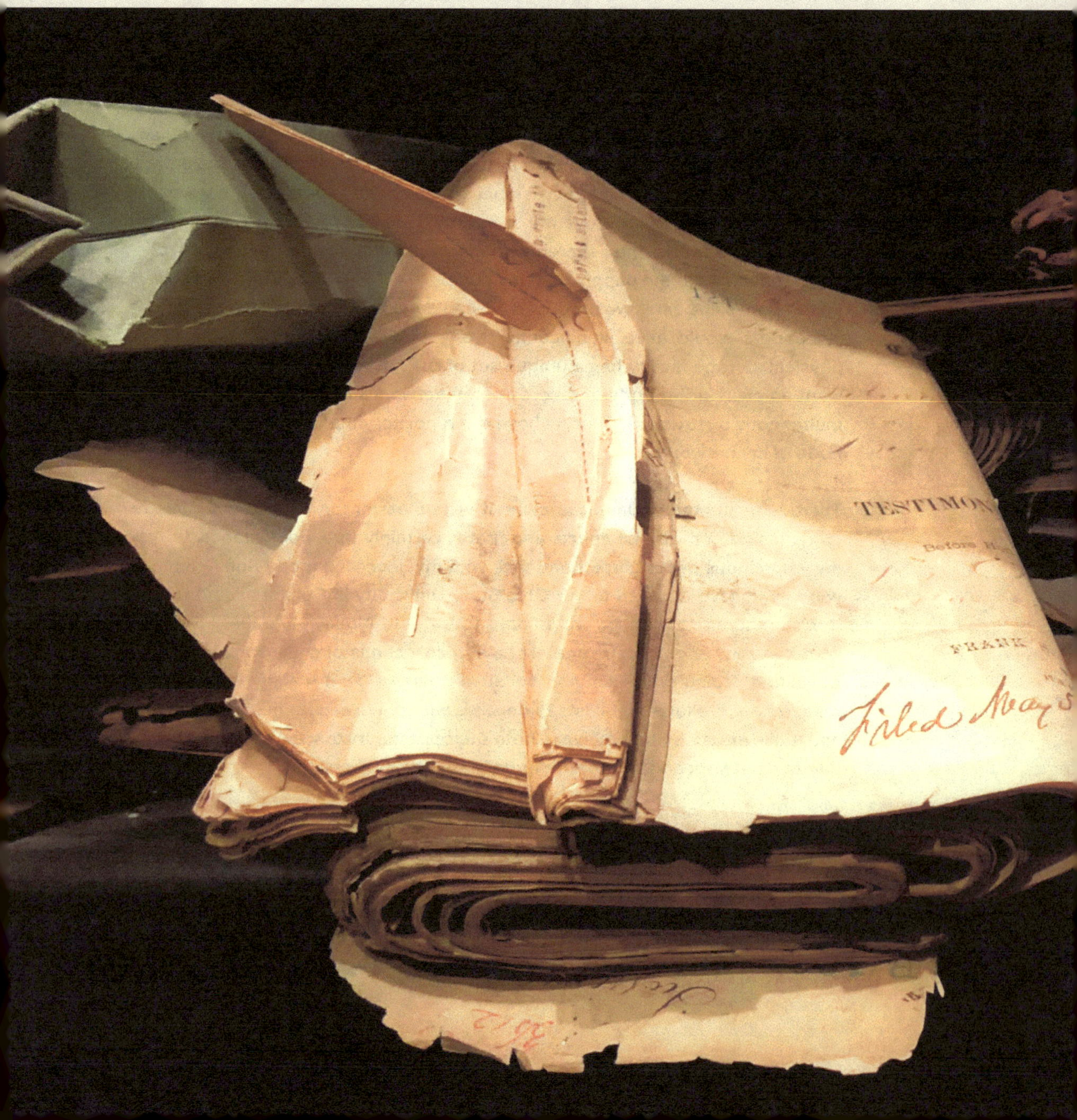

desire to amass valuable collections of archives, we can create the means to undermine that entire collection in the few hours of a major flood, devastating fire, or terrifying tornado. Collecting is too often treated as a competition, which it will always be. But we also must coordinate our work, so we can save something more valuable than a single set of records from one entity—so we can retain enough of the past to remember it into the future.

NEW YORK SUPREME COURT PAPERS IN DISARRAY (2018-04-27)

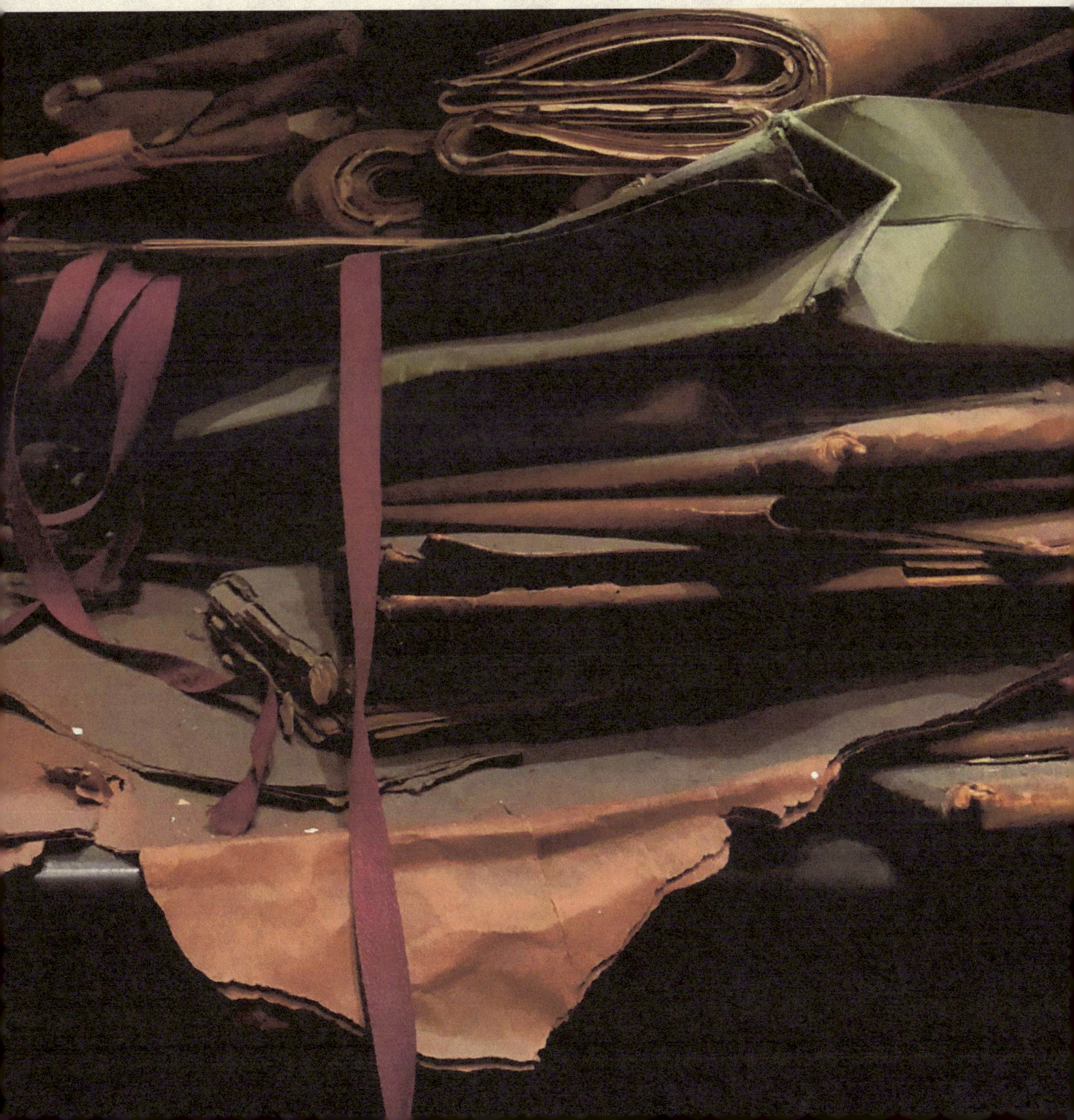

There is no state without archives.

Achille Mbembe, "The power of the archive and its limits," *Refiguring the Archive*, ed. Carolyn Hamilton (Cape Town: Clyson Printers, 2002): 23.

#archivesquotes

When Depatriation is Repatriation

The pull of the archives is strong. Archivists are sometimes so drawn to the physical aura or the intellectual allure of records under our control that we make decisions of the heart, instead of the head.

In my own work life[1], I oversee (at a stratospheric level) all the records held by the New York State Unified Court System, and I also oversee most of the library materials used in our 1514 courts across the state. The earliest extant records of the court system start in 1674,[2] and we continue to create records every day—so we have accumulated just shy of 350 years' worth of records, on the island of Manhattan. These provide a rich—though skewed—peephole into early New York City via the activities taking place in the civil and criminal courts there. And famous New Yorkers pepper these documents. We probably still hold thousands of documents bearing Aaron Burr's signature (always presented as "A.Burr").

This huge collection of records of the early and more recent English and American courts of Manhattan reaches about 13,500 cubic feet in extent. Many of these were transferred to our current physical archives, in what we call the Surrogate's Court Building, in 1911. At that time, the building was called the Hall of Records, because the City of New York had created it to store the often poorly managed records of the city, which at the time included court records. Even today, three separate archives (two of them under my general oversight) operate in this building, each holding thousands of cubic feet of records: the New York City Municipal Archives, the New York Surrogate's Court archives, and the Division of Old Records (a unit of the New York County Clerk's office).[3]

Strangely, but as expected, the Hall of Records was not a great archives—in environmental terms—for the records held by the Division of Old Records. Located on the top two floors of the building, and also in the attic just above, the archives had limited environmental controls in the winter (blistering hot radiators, known for the dryness of their heat) and none in the summer (when the heat and humidity fully occupied the rooms). After I arrived on the scene—over a century late—I added high-volume air conditioning, but all I could do was reduce further degradation.

The records had already suffered. Some sheets of paper were so brittle they had fractures in them as if they were porcelain plates dropped to the floor. The flaking of paper off folded documents was so severe that I would call accumulations of these "document dust."[4] High-quality, durable rag paper from the early 1800s was as brown as heavily acidic and acid-enslaved World War II era paper stock, and many of the folded papers had broken along their folds. The records had barely survived their confinement in the archives—which served to store, but not to protect, them.

Yet I was entranced by the records, even by their decay. I was working in an archives so dusty we could measure the depth of dust (consisting in part of soot). Many papers and parchments exhibited extreme mousechew, since the rodents of the archives feasted on all the flour paste they could find—which paste was commonly used to attach paper seals to writs of the courts. The results were ragged but nearly round holes boring through stacks of folded writs. I sometimes found parchment—likely the most durable of all archival storage media—melted into extravagant liquid shapes, apparently after resting for too long near the heat of radiators. The deep reaches of the archives were filled with hidden gin bottles, dessicated decades-old lunches, and even the remains of a single pigeon's nest.

It was every archivist's nightmare.

And that nightmare drew me in. Although many of the records were arranged in pristine—though audaciously unoriginal—order, many of the records had burst from their seams, as it were. A good number of documents had released themselves from the prison of their pine-and-canvas Willis files, which clasped bundles of folded papers together to allow them to rest on open shelving, thus avoiding the cost and inefficiency of drawers—but also opening the records up to accumulations of dust. Many of the leather-bound volumes had softened to a gentle orange-red, having been subsumed by red rot, which reduced much of the leather to a fine powder. The various degradations affecting paper documents turned them into relics barely saved from the ravages of inattention. The chaos of series of volumes, which were only occasionally identified as to type, required me to examine the volumes carefully to reassert their intended order. Even individual volumes were dispersed, having broken into two to five sections, those strewn into different corners of these rambling floors of rooms and nooks and hallways—the floors bearing the weight of many tons of paper and parchment.

The chaos was an esthetic pleasure to me, and a professional one as well. Out of this ornate chaos, I would create a complex and interconnecting system of order. My staff and I would make these records deeply findable and knowable. But, as part of my job, I was also dealing with the more recent records of the court system, maybe a million cubic feet of them (not counting the petabytes of digital records). I decided we needed to depatriate our early archival records to protect them and make them more useful to the world. As an aside, I'll note that this plan would also save the court system millions of dollars, while only marginally increasing the costs to the repositories I expected would accept these records from us.

On January 5th of 2017, part of the story of our work with these records penetrated the consciousness of tens or hundreds of thousands of people because the New York *Times* posted a story about it, complete with photographs demonstrating the wabi-sabi quality of these records and their environment.[5] The story led an archivist friend of mine to ask if I felt sad releasing the records to others. I repeated my response, in this manner, to a few colleagues in an email:

I replied that our responsibility as archivists is to the records, not our personal satisfaction. The allure of custodianship can sometimes be a bane, rather than a boon, to the records.[6]

Kate Bowers of Harvard responded with, "That last sentence should be inscribed on the hearts of all archivists before they are permitted an MS degree."[7] Of course, she did not mean this literally, but it is an important truth to remember. We need to do the best we can to manage the records under our purview, and we do this for the benefit of the potential users of those records. In some sense, we do this for the benefit of humanity as a conceptual body. We will always, as humans, be consumed by our needs and wants, but our goal, our project, our reason for being archivists is to care for records so the records can serve humankind and their broad and various needs and goals.

I had determined (honestly, just by walking through the space one summer's day) that the records and the finances of the state as a whole would be best served by depatriating the records. I counseled my superiors that this was our best option, and they agreed, so I reached out to two repositories to gauge their interest. I offered the records of the statewide courts to the New York State Archives, which likely has the best archival storage facility in our state. I offered the much more voluminous records of the courts with jurisdiction confined to Manhattan to the New York City Municipal Archives, which is developing a huge state-of-the-art archives storage facility in New York City. They both expressed their interest, because they saw how the records filled in gaps in their fonds.

The reasons for their interest reveal that we don't always initially see the world as our colleagues do. Standing on different sides of the fence, I saw one way to interpret our situation ("We are donating our records to you") and they saw another ("These records are returning home to us").

New York State law authorizes the New York State Archives to "acquire and assume the official custody" of the records of the judiciary, when they are identified as archival,[8] and that archives already holds the majority of the extant records of the early colony- and statewide court records of New York. As the archives for the government of the state of New York, the Archives was the designated home for these records, and it was already the home for many of these records' brethren—the records of three of the four offices of the Supreme Court of Judicature[9] and of seven of the eight districts of the Court of Chancery.

In the case of the New York State Municipal Archives, this sense of repatriation arose in different ways. First, many of these records began as records of the City of New York, which ran various municipal courts as part of its functions until 1977. The earliest of these courts even bore the name Mayor's Court, and the mayor himself sat on the bench as the chief judge of that court, demonstrating the undeniable connection of the court to the city. Most of the records in our archives (about 12,000 cubic feet out of the larger 13,500) were records of these dozens of courts, and most of these courts were under municipal control at some point in their history.

The city lost custody of these records in 1906 with the creation of the office of the Commissioner of Records of the County of New York, which took custody of many municipal and court records at that time.[10] In 1942, the famed mayor of New York, Fiorello La Guardia, eliminated the Commissioner of Records and transferred custody of these records to the New York County Clerk[11] as a cost-savings measure.[12] Essentially, the records remained under the control of the county, which in New York City was smaller than the city as a whole and also a component of the city. The situation changed in 1977 with the creation of the New York State Unified Court System, which merged all the courts of the state—from tiny village courts to our highest court, the Court of Appeals—into one statewide court system, an entity that became the revised and expanded judicial branch of New York State government.

At that point, all the county clerks in New York City (each of whom served as the clerk of their branch of the Supreme Court) became part of the Unified Court System, and the court records held by the New York County Clerk became state government records. The archives of the early courts of the City of New York became the clear property of the State of New York. But we in the court system decided in 2015 that it would be best for the records, for the court system, for the city, and especially for users if we could transfer custody of these records back to the city.

This is also why we depatriated records to the State Archives: so we could repatriate them, so we could restore a fonds that had never before existed in the same location, so we could recreate a universe, to make it as whole as we could make it and as whole as it could ever be. Our goal was repatriation and depatriation simultaneously. We needed to take the proper steps to protect the records and to make them easier for users to access.

Soon after we transferred records to the New York State Archives, the archivists there and the researchers who went there to examine them began to rewrite history, or at least re-understand it. They began to unwhitewash the American Revolution as it pertained to the seizure of Loyalists' real property in New York State; they quickly discovered that this republic of ours, based on the importance of the rule of law, rushed decisions to strip the property rights of Loyalists—en masse, dozens of people at a time. We learned what the world actually was and who our forebears truly used to be.

And this means the plan worked. The archives increased in value as the records were used ever more deeply, and the records gained the opportunity to survive a bit longer into the future, so that people yet born could learn something from them that none of us has yet learned.

We keep archives for the future. They were created in the past, and we use them in the present, but they are meant as just one way we can change the future. Sometimes we do this only by better understanding the past and sometimes by learning enough to transform the essential body of human knowledge.

Our purpose as archivists is not small, and it is not well understood by others. We are here to make the past knowable and to achieve a better, a deeper, future. And sometimes we do this by giving away the records we have and might still want to keep. We do this after we have arranged, described, and contextualized them after thousands of hours of human endeavor. We prepare the records for use and understanding. We do this as archivists do. We create structure in a deconstructed world.

Archivists need to accept that we, as individuals and as discrete organizations, are not always the best custodians of the records we currently keep. Accepting that doesn't require sadness or regret. Accepting that means accepting our purpose. We find the best records to keep. We find the best place to keep them. We ensure people can find them.

We do not change the world. We give the world to others so they can change it for us.

Although smells, at least outside of a controlled environment, are ephemeral, that does not mean that olfactory information is necessarily "lost." Scholars in many other disciplines have argued that the ephemeral can be archival too, without being subjected to traditional archival principles.

Anna Chen, "Perfume and Vinegar: Olfactory Knowledge, Remembrance, and Recordkeeping," *The American Archivist* 79:1 (Spring/Summer 2016): 111.

#archivesquotes #scent

Necessary Nothings

[A SHORT STORY]

PAPER

She could believe in the beauty of paper, but not for the fibers themselves, or how the page could age slowly, if carefully, into a field of textures, new colors arising out of whiteness into a muslin, how a slanted light through a windowpane could put that flat world into relief. Instead, she saw in paper the beauty of holding. At the moment of that thought, she gazed not so much at the paper itself as at the ink sunk into it. She imagined the wetness so black that it struck out the paper's white light, and then she imagined how the ink dried, the quickness of it, how the shiny black wetness sunk into dullness and flattened out, all in a second. She imagined the suddenness of it. As sudden as—

But everything was sudden. She never expected it, whatever it might be, and yet it fell upon her in an instant. A neighbor's cough through the wall. The appearance below her of a rat, followed by its saunter over, under, and around the subway tracks. That one woman she did not even see as she crossed the middle of the street at a slant, but then the woman spoke softly (a suddenness), and she twirled into another angled walking and saw her there:

Black, tall but slight, maybe only slender, delicate features, thin graceful fingers, one hand of them quivering around a burning cigarette, and she spoke,

"Could, I am wondering, well, you see, maybe—"

The woman cut herself off as the reply became a soft,

"I'm sorry," an explanation, a sorrow not suppressed enough for city living, the poor trans woman, how does she cope? then a trailing off of thought, until a sudden thought she whispered sotto voce and away from the woman, in the direction of her morning's commute:

"I am Amy. I am loved."

Hers was an act of convincing.

She remembered the first hole she had seen that iron gall ink had cut through a sheet of paper, how its darkness opened the page, created a window, let in the light.

ELECTRICITY

Everything is digital, she thought to herself—at least electric. If my brain stops sending electrical messages to my body, it all stops. Stop thinking! she thought to herself.

Actually, Petrie stopped her thinking—another diatribe of his:

"CDs!? You're going to preserve your life on CDs? A whole box of them, too? Why not just ramp up the capacity and go to DVDs? An extra letter there—they'll probably last at least 50% longer. I think I saw a commercial for it."

"Petrie."

"Amy?"

"Maybe quieter."

"Maybe nothing?"

"I mean, c'mon. It's not your first day on the job. These things happen. People think things will last. You know the game."

"Yep. Everyone's an idiot, and I have to deal with them."

"I mean, have you even looked at the data yet?"

"Not data, Amy: records, real records."

"It's the Science Fiction Club records, for goodness' sakes."

"So?"

"It's not the end of the world."

"Isn't that what science fiction is about?"

"Petrie..."

"Okay, I'll get back to work. It's just I can't take it."

WINDOWS

He can't take it? He doesn't even have to listen to himself. I'm sure he doesn't. Or he listens to it as music. He can't hear the words, only their sounds.

She knew she was supposed to enjoy people, but there was this constant suddenness to them. Paper never jumped out of a box and started yelling about bit rot or the coming post-apocalyptic world when all of our fast and easy digital information instantly becomes worthless and the history of humankind is wiped out, except for one old woman they call Alexandria because—

Stop!

She yelled the thought at herself. She thought it as a yell.

And she stopped.

What's the point of being the head of a department when you can't even get out of reference duty? I mean, I like helping people and talking to them. I want them to find something. I wait for that treasure—overused word—that find—to turn up. "Find" is good, some nudge of a piece of information that finishes a puzzle, or starts it, just a spark they can turn into a fire. Something to stop the inexorableness of the coming plague.

I just can't stand watching them look inside boxes. We need records in the form of videogames. Records with some motion to them. It would be just a step away from emotion. Something human. Maybe a laugh. A gasp.

Oh. He's scratching himself again.

An old man. Too old. She couldn't imagine his age. She tried to remember. Late eighties, at least. Frail, but with a sturdiness to his bones, and his face. Firm nose. Wiry fingers and slow, too, but still fluid. It's as if he moved in slow motion. Everything worked naturally, just slowly. Fine white hair, in waves off his head. The hairs collected all the rays of bulblight in the room.

We need windows. It would be good to see a bird sometimes.

But the light. Bad for paper, bad for records, bad for books. But we still have to see.

We still want to see.

LIGHT

She walked home in a swale of sunlight, the whole way down the avenue. Could not be rid of it, and she didn't want to. She loved the bright, the warm, how heavy with heat the weather was that time of the year. She loved the look sunlight gave the world. How it almost hurt to see.

And she was done! At least for the day. At least for now. Until tomorrow. She remembered being a student thrilled at the possibility of doing what she was now doing. Was it really the same job? She thought it was a calling. Or a visitation. Floating Mary, a fan of light from the right corner of the page (it's not an image for canvas), arms outstretched, palms turned upward but slanted toward the ground, toward her, toward the one being visitated.

Archives is the opium of the archivists.

Drank the whole glass of it, she thought. I drank the whole sweet glassful. In one gulp. And has the world changed? No. But it's changed me.

The whole time these thoughts were juggling through her head, a thread of an idea wriggled through it, a wariness. She didn't want to see her again. Not that she was scary. She didn't scare her at all. She just reminded her of something.

She shows me who I didn't become.

It was too sharp a thought.

She reminds me what I want to be.

I'm giving myself a pass. Can't do that. I need some spine.

She smelled a whiff of vinegar.

Vinegar syndrome: the autocatalytic point. The point at which acetate film has degraded so much it begins to eat itself. The chemicals that begin that process then reproduce themselves. It's a geometrical process of decay. A speeding-up.

Just like my thoughts: thinking creates thoughts, then multiplication, autocatalysis. I can't even pronounce that word. But it's just like me: I should call myself Autocatalytic Catherine—good use for my middle name. So Catholic. Good for someone who's waiting for Mary. There's that scent again.

Salad dressing, she thought.

She needed to get home.

CANINE

She fiddled with the can of dog food, the can opener not quite grabbing right inside the rim. It was a problem of aim, of focus. Marcus was running around her feet. The anticipation of small dogs at the possibility of food was enough to make her move herself out of her bed every morning.

It's good when the can opener doesn't work, when I can't get it to work for a second. Gives me a tiny space in my day, a waiting, a breath. I need that little bit of space between all the doing. I need that gap. All the tiny voids in the day that stop me for a second. Space to think.

Marcus was jumping, forefeet landing against her shins, tail whipping at the empty air enough to make something of it. A few swift turns of the knob, and the can's top tilted open. Quick scoops of a meatlike substance into his metal dish, that dish laid onto the floor, and Marcus was within the envelope of his own form of zen: Frantic gulps of food, his snout and tail (both ends of him) out of control, joy.

It could be worse, she thought. I could have a cat. Or I could have named Marcus Dog. Rick's great idea...Yep, naming him instead after an emperor-philosopher was the right choice! How could that ever be used against me?

She plopped herself backwards onto the bed and considered the ceiling.

I bet Rick'll be late. That's his style. And what kind of name is Rick for someone named Eric? Or why do we think that is strange? The more nothing makes sense, the more we believe in it.

She lay there, on the bed, eyes following the shadows the light through the windows cast onto the ceiling, comfortable in the warm light, easy in her little nothing time, until Rick made it home.

FOUNTAIN

She ruminated on the idea that sitting at the reference desk, overseeing patrons looking through her archives, could allow time for her little pauses. But it was impossible to accept, because at any time there could be a suddenness.

"Please."

The voice startled her. How did he get so close so quickly without my seeing him?

"Oh. Yes?"

"Could you find the letter now?"

"'The letter'? Mr. Blumenthal."

"Yes. From my brother. The one I wrote you about."

Mr. Blumenthal was anything but unprepared. He had written her thirteen times before he appeared in person. She counted the emails over to be sure. He worked out all the details far ahead of time. Even arrived right at the time he had planned: 12:15. Who would choose 12:15? Why not just go to lunch? And, yes, now she had remembered the letter. She knew its importance, but there were so many details he had told her. She forgot that she'd figured out he asked for everything in the order he'd originally written to her about them.

"Yes, yes, I remember. I can get it right away. Do you want the rest of the correspondence, or just that box?"

"One letter only."

"Well, we only bring out the whole box. I can get it now."

"Then the whole box then."

As she retrieved the box, she wondered about the significance of the letter. When she placed the box on his table, he thanked her and his eyes creased a little, almost as if he were peering at her more closely than usual, trying to read her. Probably, he was just thinking about the letter.

From her vantage point back at the desk—she called it her aerie, because it was slightly elevated from the tables laid out before her—she watched Mr. Rosenthal a little more attentively herself. She wanted to watch him find the letter. First, he pulled a pen out of his pocket and took off the cap.

She took herself through the steps she used to allow herself to let him to break that rule: "ONLY Pencils." Pens are permanent. Pencils' marks you can erase. Well, they are his papers. Any mark he makes on the papers is a mark he might have made when he had them himself. Sure, sure, people might assume the mark appeared sometime before he donated them, but would that really jeopardize their integrity? Anyway, he's an old man, he's used to fountain pens... Okay, fountain pens are really bad. But he came all the way from Germany, and this is the first time he's ever used his own papers. And he's an old man. He's got other concerns. He was lucky to make it out of Germany as a young man—why would I want to give him grief now?

She didn't quite consider hers an intellectual decision.

LISTERINE

Petrie was at it again.

"Why am I even doing this? I pull off all these disk images, and the backup we have is two blocks away?"

"Petrie, you know we're working on this. Everything doesn't happen all at once."

"Then why do you always say, "'How come everything happens all at once?'?"

"You know that's different."

"Y'know, I've got an idea. Why don't we just spray hard drives with Listerine to eliminate viruses too? Saves time, more efficient, smells good."

(Smells good?)

"Petrie, we do the best we can when we can, and we look for ways to do things better. And I'm going to assume that we're doing better than Listerine right now, so be glad about our progress."

"Do you even care?"

"Petrie..."

"Sorry. Sorry. I know you do. I just get upset."

"Maybe too upset?"

"Maybe too upset."

"Thanks, Petrie. You know we need you, but sometimes I need a little space too."

"I know. It's just a bad day. The whole X-Files revival is just going to drive me crazy."

Don't I even care? Isn't it obvious? I mean, he said I did. I must have to prove it more. I have to make it happen. I care—I just have to make it tangible.

FLOWERS

Mr. Blumenthal was leaving. He said he was done. And so he was. She'd forgotten the letter was the last item he'd written her about. As she walked over to his table, she noticed he was sad, a little teary.

"Mr. Blumenthal, are you all right?"

"Oh, it is just the letter. A long time ago."

"Do you miss him?"

"For so long. He never came out. We don't know what happened to him. It's the only words we have left of him."

"He died? In the war?"

"Yes. Never came out. They killed him."

"I'm so sorry."

"It is fine. It was a long time ago. I was still young. Didn't even know what death was yet."

"Mr. Blumenthal—if I could—what was the letter about?"

"It was about nothing. Very short. He went on a trip to Austria. Wrote us about his time there. Mostly the opera. He loved opera."

"How old was he?"

"Younger than my grandchildren are now. It was a long time ago. He is why I returned."

"Why you went back to Germany?"

"Yes."

"You went back after the war..."

"I waited first. But, yes, after the war."

"And your uncle was killed by them?"

"People killed him because they said he was not German, that he didn't belong there. But we don't know who killed him. Or when. Or where. But we know that."

"But, then, why did you go back?"

"Because they said I wasn't a German. They said we weren't German. But it was our country. We were the Germans, too. It was not just them."

"It must have been hard, though—going back."

"Death is hard. The deaths were hard. I went back so I could live in my country. I went back to create it over again."

"Was it worth it?"

"Life is worth it. It is hard, but it is worth it. We learned to create life again."

THING

She couldn't believe she didn't know this story already. She didn't realize how little she knew about him. She knew his history, but why didn't she wonder why he returned? What was she focused on?

I didn't focus on the thing. I focused on the description of the records, the little things we make up to tell people what the records are. I know they're not the thing. I always knew that.

How did I forget?

ELLA

When she said goodbye, she realized what she needed to recognize at that moment: that she would never see him again, that he had been merely thirteen emails to her, then he became thirteen emails and a fountain pen. She hadn't really listened to him. (When did she stop really listening?)

After he thanked her, she thanked him for everything she could think of. For being so prepared. For donating his papers. For the work he had done. For leaving his papers in America. For being such a good researcher. And she hugged him, wrapping her arms around his slight frame, and holding him gently but tight.

He kissed her on the cheek and said goodbye again.

She stood there, for a few minutes, in the research room, barely moving, alone. She felt her body without moving it. She felt her heart beating, her lungs breathing—she was sure she could feel the pulse of blood through her arms. She was out of breath.

All of a sudden, the world surrounded her.

On the walk home, she moved more deliberately, she felt the slightest breeze pushing up the avenue, she noticed a few birds in the trees, and the song of birds, and the weird cleft fan that was every leaf of every gingko she passed. She smelled the urine, wondered if it were canine or human—or both. She heard a man yell at another and run after him, but she didn't turn to see. She saw a taxi driver sweating at a stoplight. She saw a cat cross the street, and she imagined where around there it might live.

She saw the woman from yesterday, and the woman saw her and turned away. She jogged after the woman, calling out,

"Please. Wait a second. Can I talk to you?"

The woman stopped, she turned, sweat glistened on her shoulder, she waited. She wore her name on a little chain around her neck: Ella.

Amy caught up to her.

She had no idea what she was going to say.

These ideas around identity, self-representation, and memory apply not only to the writing of self, but also to the documentation of self. A personal fonds is the creator's memory passed on —his legacy.

Carolyn Harris, "Paper Memories, Presented Selves: Original Order and the Arrangement of the Donald G. Simpson Fonds at York University," *Archivaria* 74 (Fall 2012): 210.

#archivesquotes

Memory & Evidence

Memory is often evidence. Courts support the idea of memory as evidence. A witness testifies, and the witness is believed, unless other evidence undermines the testimony or until the opposing counsel interrogates the witness.

But memory is slippery, fluid. It changes with time. The mind flushes details from its system, retains the highlights of a life and reduces the general activities of that life to conflated memories: this was the hallway of my high school, this was the beach from which I swam out into the ocean, this was the face of my mother.

Archivists speak of memory and see archives as one way we concretize and retain memory. They speak of collective memory, some huge storehouse of knowledge shared across a network of humans, each of whom represents a neuron in the great human mind, but each of which knows only some of the shared memory of humanity or some connected set of people. We are each a neuron in a huge collective mind, yet that raggedy mind—filled with facts and fictions—remains unreliable. Because of the inherent unreliability of the human mind and its concomitant memory, we understand our collective memory to be built upon a horde of data we never know the full reaches of.

Archives form the foundation—we might say the fonds—of this shared memory system, because archives provide reliability, authenticity, trustworthiness—all features many humans personally lack. And so we hear from the voices of archivists of their concept of evidence, one where evidence is believable, where the process of creating and keeping the records ensures a truth—whatever that is—that verifies our memories.

Listen, for instance, to Hilary Jenkinson—

> I am not to attempt here an exposition of the value of archives, but if I were asked to define the creed of the archivist in four words I should say "the sanctity of evidence." [1]

—and David Bearman—

> But, just as a surgeon might prefer to seek refuge in the justification of relieving pain, I suggest that archivists justify their activity as ensuring evidence.[2]

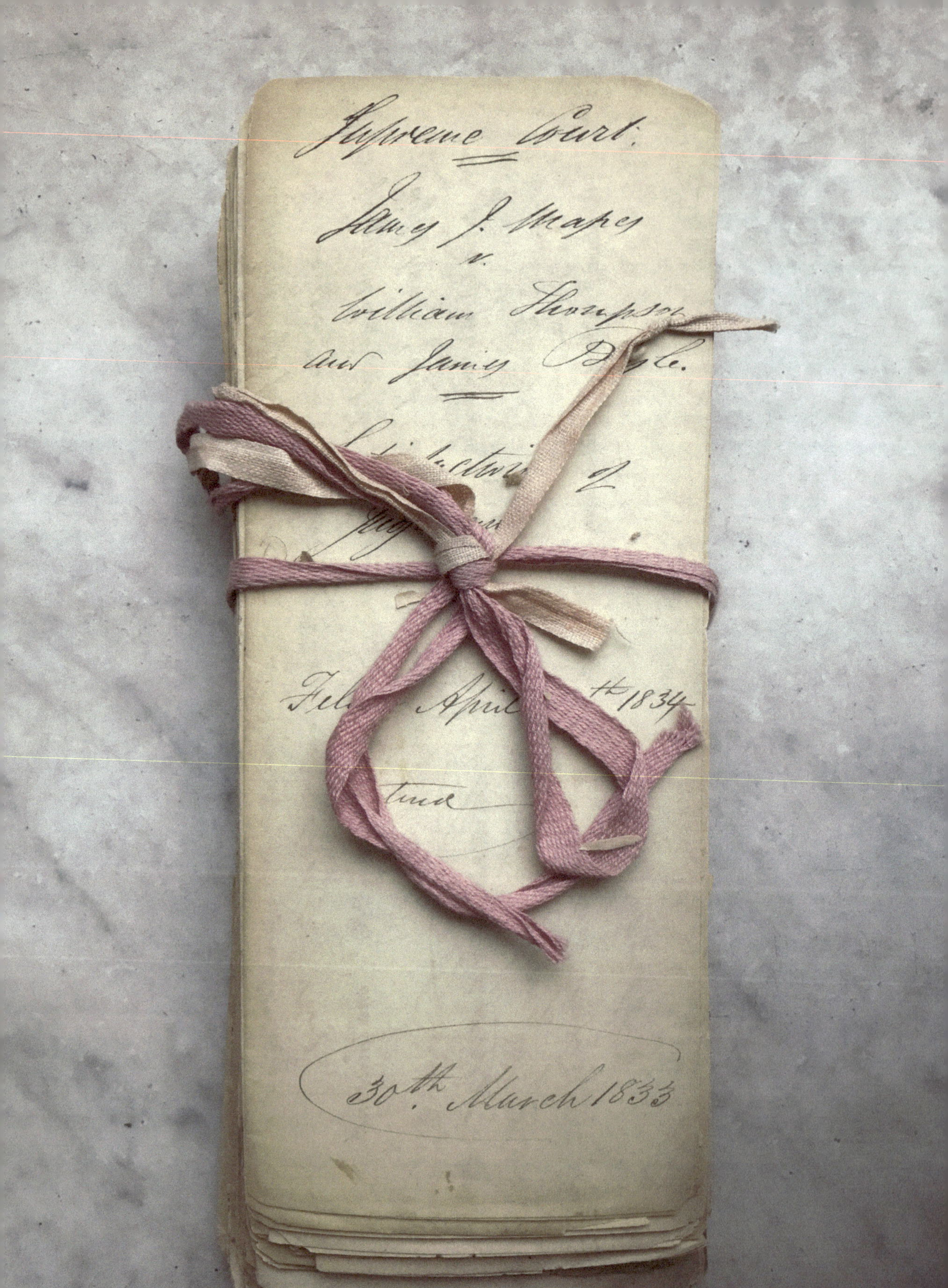

SUPREME COURT OF JUDICATURE SATISFACTION OF JUDGMENT (1833)

—and William J. Maher—

What is, in fact, so troubling about the many pseudo-archives now being established is that they frequently lack several of the very core archival functions. In some cases, it is that they constitute private and idiosyncratic collections developed ex post facto, and thus are far from the contextually based organic bodies of evidence that comprise most of the archives and manuscript collections among the members of SAA.[3]

Bill Maher gets to the point: archivists believe in evidence when they know records have been created in a system that requires accurate information, includes oversight of the records creators, and manages the records as a valued resource. Evidence is not a figment of the mind, something we think up or hear or taste and sometimes can recall a year later. Evidence is not truly memory, at least not to the archivist. Evidence derives from a system that must create reliable information to function. Evidence is what we make and can save and protect. Evidence is not what we remember.

Yet we continue to think of it as memory, because memory is the closest natural analog to a record. Memory is the remnants of human experience held within a human body. A memory is a stored thought, some fact one has lived or heard or read. Evidence, though, is a stored act, preserved on some material that may or may not endure as long as the evidence is needed but that we can depend on to support human activity as necessary.

Maher, speaking of archivists, says something that pushes archivy even further towards an ecclesiatic reverence toward evidence:

We are not information professionals like librarians—we are evidence professionals.[4]

His is a good thought. It forces archivists to consider the clear requirement that people must be able to believe in the archives they are consulting—even when they know the archives are full of lies. As we all know, some systems of recordkeeping are reliable as records but false with regard to the facts they maintain. Many organizations and loose associations of humans are based on belief in either falsehoods or unconfirmable information. The system itself may be truthful, in that it documents the methods for producing and vetting the information, but that doesn't mean the information is truth. It's unlikely much information is purely true.

That, I believe, is the allure of memory as a concept in archives. Evidence may be fake, and memories may be faulty. We may even convince ourselves to remember something that never happened. Or we may have a clear memory of something we never witnessed, because we have taken into our bodies the spouted memory of a reliable witness. I call these rememories, memories transferred to us second-hand—which are often the clearest memories of our childhood.

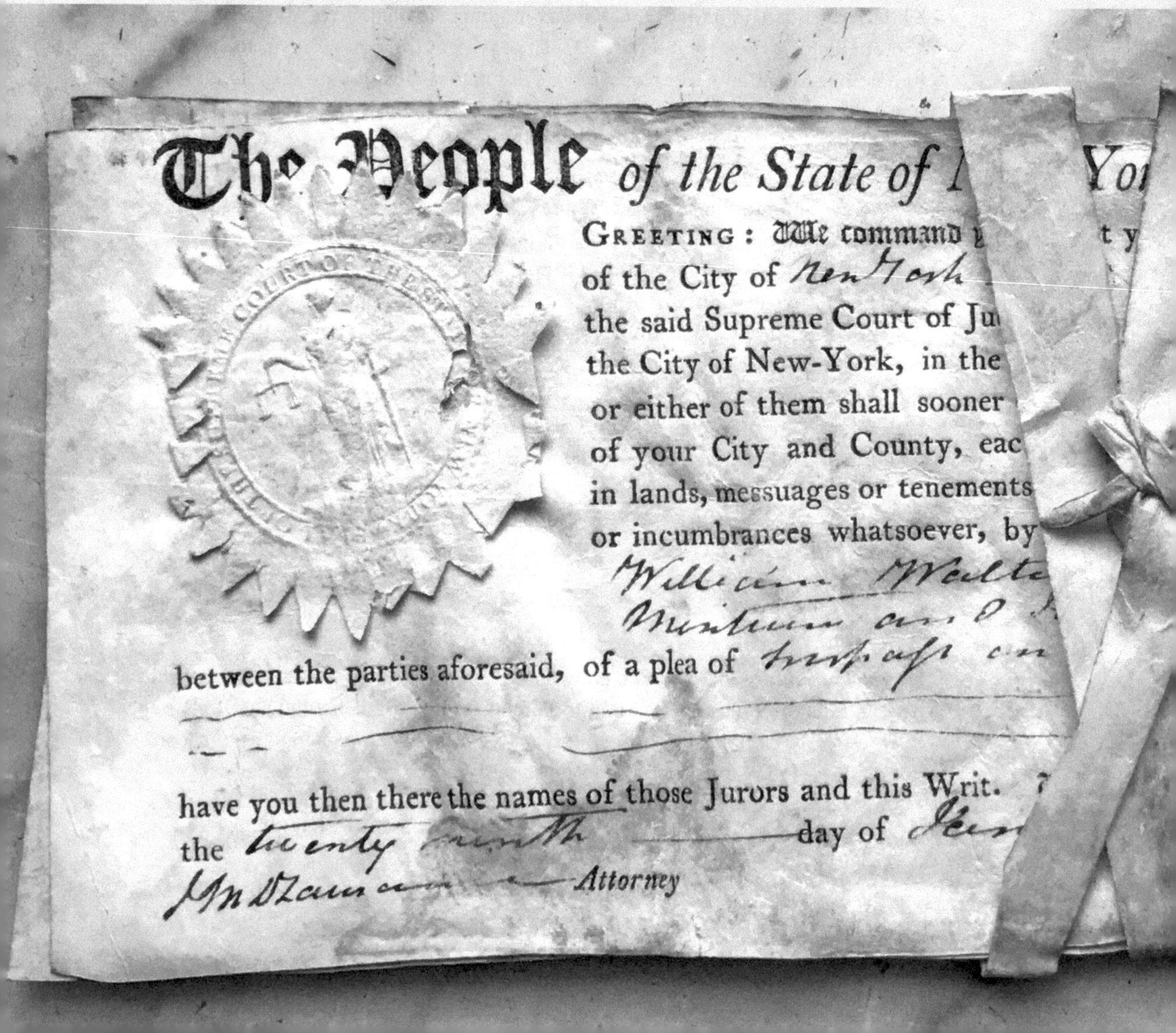

We love memories, even the painful ones, because they inhabit us, they define, they are—truly—all that we know. Evidence is good and hard and reliable, and we can sometimes trust the data within it, but memory is breathed into and out of our bodies. We love most what we carry always within ourselves.

I once believed I had a conversation in Pittsburgh—my memory told me this—only to learn I was in Bethlehem all along.[5]

NEW YORK SUPREME COURT OF JUDICATURE PARCHMENT WRITS TIED TOGETHER WITH PARCHMENT (29 JUNE 1803)

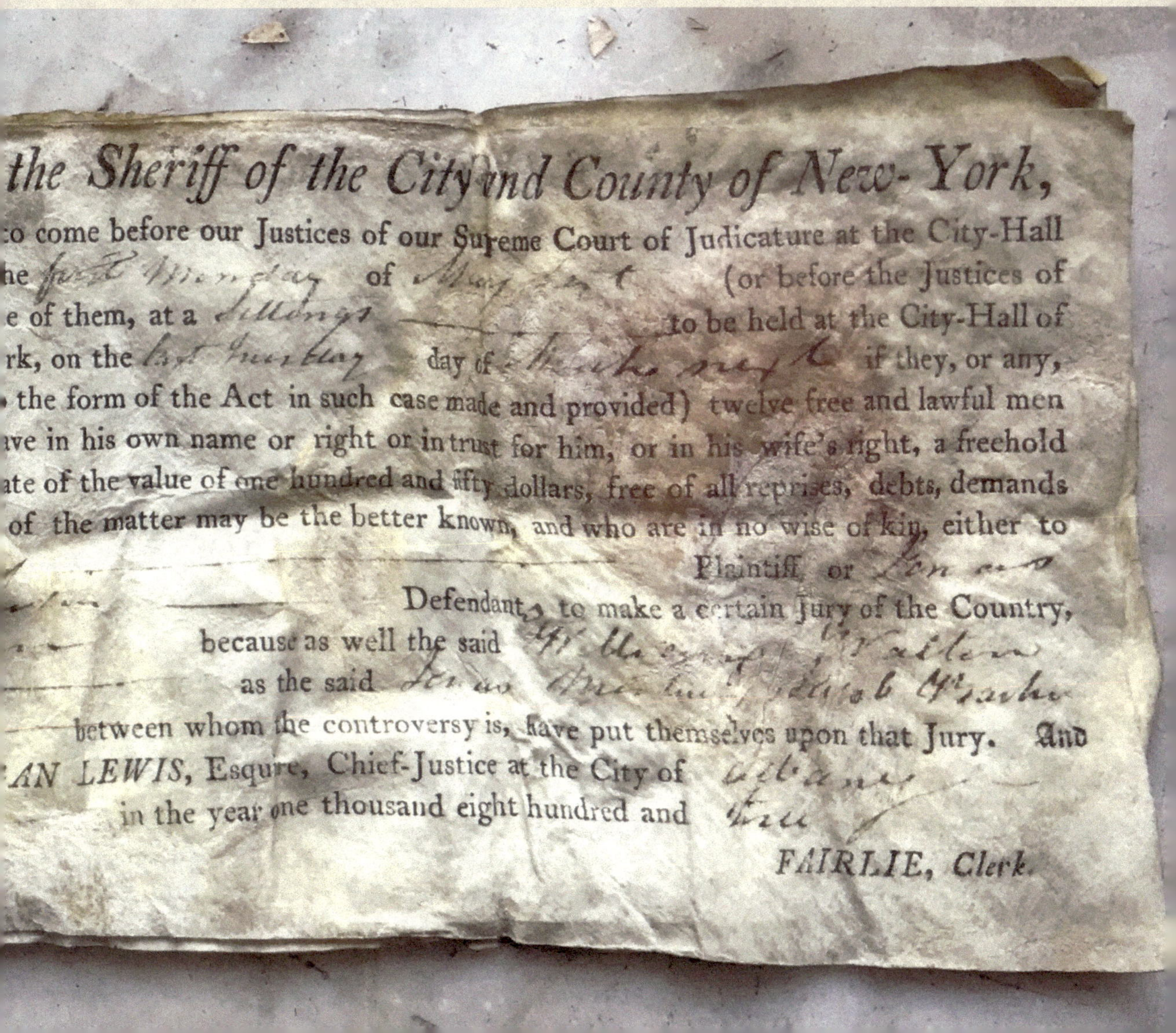

the Sheriff of the City and County of New-York,
to come before our Justices of our Supreme Court of Judicature at the City-Hall
he of (or before the Justices of
e of them, at a to be held at the City-Hall of
rk, on the day of if they, or any,
the form of the Act in such case made and provided) twelve free and lawful men
ve in his own name or right or in trust for him, or in his wife's right, a freehold
ate of the value of one hundred and fifty dollars, free of all reprises, debts, demands
of the matter may be the better known, and who are in no wise of kin, either to
Plaintiff or
Defendant, to make a certain Jury of the Country,
because as well the said
as the said
between whom the controversy is, have put themselves upon that Jury. And
AN LEWIS, Esquire, Chief-Justice at the City of
in the year one thousand eight hundred and
FAIRLIE, Clerk.

At its deepest, most fundamental level, archives assumes a genuine faith in humanity, a faith that there will be a future and generations to which archives will matter.

Scott Cline, "'To the Limit of Our Integrity': Reflections on Archival Being," *The American Archivist* 72:2 (Fall/Winter 2009): 334.

#archivalfaith #archivalbeing #archivesquotes

Records as Opposed to Archives as Opposed to Records

Records are not naturally archival. Only human intervention in the form of a decision transforms records into archives. And human intervention can also reverse that decision. Just as we appraise records, we can reappraise them.

The archivist,[1] however, starts within a state of nothingness. Or each archivist's entire universe of documentation lies before them, even if as-yet-unknown, even if likely not wholly knowable. The various universes an archivist might encounter differ. One archivist may have the sole responsibility of managing the records of their own institution; another may be required to acquire those pure archives and, in addition, collect records documenting multiple aspects of human activity—as well as rare books and ephemera. The world may be finite, but the possibilities within it are infinite.

Deciding what records may be honored with the designation "archival" begins with the assumptions and biases rattling inside the archivist's head. We cannot escape our preconceptions, so we must control them, by dint of will. For instance, most archivists likely believe that age is one marker of archives; if a record is old, then it is archival—or, at least, likely so. In this syllogism,[2] we accept that records of any slice of the past are less abundant than records today, then we posit that the relative paucity of records suggests that that era is likely not documented to the degree to which our own age is, and thus we conclude that we must save the record to ensure we have retained reasonably robust documentation of that past.

The problem with syllogism is it requires us to make assumptions that lead us to a destination that may not be the correct one. The constant problem with this logical formulation is that it begins with assumptions (two premises), which may or may not be true—even as they are believed to be. Equating age with value tricks us into ignoring, at least to a degree, the data in the record itself. Since we are nearing a century since archivists began announcing we have too many records to manage reasonably, we need to be skeptical about easy answers to appraisal conundrums.[3] I have sat in appraisal meetings arguing with colleagues that records from the 1940s do not constitute records of archival value merely because of their date of creation. We must always focus on the value of the records' data. The planet can lose metric tons of records from the 1940s and still retain a reasonable level of documentation of humanity. We simply do not need everything.

Regardless of the level of intellectual rigor and procedural precision we might employ, any attempt at appraisal is a crap shoot. Appraisal is the act of determining today the value of parts of yesterday to the world come tomorrow. Appraisal is an act of faith and futurism. We imagine a future in which these records under consideration still exist, and we consider if people will use them frequently and deeply enough to justify their continued existence. And how do we determine the needs of the future? By extrapolating based on the use of such records today and by trying to imagine new uses that could be made of these records.

Yet what the past tells us most clearly is that our assumptions about the future are often incorrect. We may over- or underestimate use. New ideas for using records will appear in the future, and the volume of these new ideas will always exceed archivists' imaginations about such use—because we are always outnumbered by the quantity of potential users, and because we are generally not using the records ourselves. We did not imagine the data-heavy uses of records often made today. We did not conceive of historians collecting masses of unstructured data that they would then give structure to, thus creating richer ways to understand the past. We did not imagine the computer age. We did not conceive of studying all the records—held by multiple repositories and government agencies—about the female head librarians of the branch libraries of New York Public Library to create a rich social history of those women.

Actually, one of us did imagine the last of these[4] because that is the focus of the research of Bob Sink, formerly the institutional archivist of the New York Public Library, and now retired. Archivists themselves can be researchers, and in being such they can imagine new uses of records, but having all archivists be researchers is unlikely to improve appraisal decisions. First, we will still be individual humans thinking in our own ways; we will not gain the imaginations of all potential researchers just by being one ourselves. The real issue is even deeper. Most research cannot take place in but a single repository. Just as the universe of records is bigger than any one archives can manage, so the universe of a single research project almost always exceeds the range of a single repository.

That is why the archivist must always be an existentialist when it comes to appraisal: "I can't appraise records. I'll appraise records."[5] "Ever tried. Ever failed.

No matter. Try again. Fail again. Fail better." [6] We have to accept the likelihood of failure without being consumed by despair.

Archival appraisal is an audacious act. When appraising, we make decisions about matters of life and death (though only for records). We transform a mere record—a concretized set of data documenting purported facts—into an archive. We designate a record to become part of that most exalted category of record: archival, and thus permanent. Because of the power permanence asserts on the future and the cost of that permanence to our organizations, we must do this carefully to justify our decisions.

Yet our decisions may not always stand. The sad truth about appraisal is that others may undo our conclusion. A record one person marked as archival may become something else: a record to discard, a record to transfer to another organization, a record to sell. Those who come after us may symbolically countersign our appraisal reports—or tear them up. An archival record today may become non-archival tomorrow.

One reason for this is that other archivists come to different conclusions about the records. Another is that the circumstances and facts that guided the original decision have changed. When an archives begins to run out of space—when space becomes more precious—the records themselves must demonstrate their value even more clearly. Archives, you see, are archives only in certain contexts; if the context changes, then the value of the record also fluctuates—up, down, or even sideways. A little acknowledged truth is that no record is purely archival. No record is archival in any contexts. A record that is archival to one repository has no archival value in another.

Take the case of the journals of Lewis and Clark on their explorations across the North American continent. Given the historical import of their work and the findings they revealed to most of the world—though definitely not all—you might assume that these records are simply and purely archival. But that cannot be the case. A record is archival only in the context in which it is kept. Thus a record may have clear archival value in an abstract sense, yet have no concrete archival value in the context of most repositories. If, for instance, someone approached a business archives and asked the archivist there if they would care to acquire the original journals of Lewis and Clark, they would likely turn away the offer, because the records would have no archival value in their corporate context. Just as records carry meaning because of the context of their creation and later use, records carry archival value in the context of the archives assessing that value.

Also, appraisal is always a process of subjective analysis. We can, and certainly should, create objective criteria to guide our appraisal decisions—measurable

SCRAPS OF MAYOR'S COURT RECORDS (2017-01-24)

criteria created to make sense in the context of our specific archives—but subjectivity is unavoidable. And objectivity is often litigated rather than affirmed by subsequent archivists. I see every archivist as a sturdy link in a never-ending chain, one connected to the next as each of us assumes the responsibility from a predecessor and then transfers that responsibility to a successor. A break in the chain (via subpar storage, theft, a disaster, or even outright abandonment of the archives) can eliminate a record or set of records forever—so we usually work assiduously to ensure the protection of our archives. But sometimes we do not, because sometimes we are the link in the chain that disagrees with all the preceding links.

This fact underlines the subjectivity of archives. We don't always agree with each other's appraisal decisions, which is good. Disagreement leads to discussion (in the best of cases), which leads to better and more nuanced decisions. This has been true in most of my appraisal work, which almost always included multiple people evaluating individual series or fonds of records and arguing about whether they were archival—and to what degree they were. My experience, however, was synchronic: five or six people sat around a table and debated the analysis one of us had written.

When we decide to veto a decision of a predecessor, our argument is with an absent past. We make the decision based on current thinking and conditions— the latter often having to do with the value of shelf space as compared to the value of the records resting thereon. In such reappraisals, we question past decisions, consider them in our current context, and decide if decisions of the past still hold true for the future.

Often enough, we rescind the archival imprimatur given to the records—but only as they relate to us in our environment. After transforming archives back into mere records, we often do something counterintuitive: we search for archives where these records may become archival again. We try to transform something that was once a mere record and then an archive and once again a record back into an archive. We struggle for redemption—because we believe there still may exist a sliver of value for the record, a corner of humanity where it is indeed an archive.

How many people can say, “I get to empower people to make good decisions”?

Karen Jamison Trivette, “Episode 86: The Connections between Then and Now” (Nicole Milano),” *An Archivist’s Tale* (recorded 21 September 2019, released 12 October 2019).

#archivesquotes

Remembering as a Form of Forgetting

A record, any record, is an amalgam of rememberedness and forgottenness—but we usually believe, if unconsciously so, that records embody only that first characteristic. We believe a record documents an activity, giving it substance long after that event has occurred. If we pause for a moment and consider the facts of a record's production, we will realize a record is always nothing more than the simulacrum of an event or transaction. It is never the thing itself, except insofar as it is a different thing itself. The record always leaves out information, just as a memory in the mind reduces the complexity of the event, eliminates ancillary data, and focuses on the main action at hand or whatever most impressed itself into the mind of the rememberer.

Which is to say: Records aren't complete. If I ask you at this moment to tell me the event in your life that touches you the most, that connects you to the immanence of ineffable reality, you can tell me the story—given a few moments to identify it within your memory banks. Yet you cannot recount the whole story. Most of the occurrences of your life have already been forsaken by the layer of memory you retain. You will tell a version of the story; but you will not recreate the event, not even the full contours of the event.

So it is with records. They are fulsome, we might say, but only because *fulsome* carries with it two opposing meanings. Yet a record need not be a full accounting of something. Such a process would be crippled by inefficiency.

We might wonder why we believe in the record—putting aside temporarily the reality that we believe anything to whatever degree we are not biased against believing it. The *Jenkinsonian*[1] ideal is that the record—let's say the archive, to make this more precise—is evidence, so long as an unbroken chain of custody ensures it remains inviolate, whole, and unaltered in its essential elements (its meaning and content) by the progress of time. But changelessness is hardly the only element we need to forego doubt and render ourselves heavy with the burden of belief.

We believe in records because we assume, sometimes with adequate evidence, that most recordmaking processes are naturally accurate—or lean heavily towards accuracy and truth—merely because reliable information is necessary to support a business process. Even in the context of an individual human, that human is likely to write a reasonably accurate account of their life because they want the record to remember in place of their vacillating memory itself. They need and desire memory firmer than that of a human, memory recorded on something less malleable than human brain tissue.

Memory is tricky. The record is hard and fast. We tell ourselves these things.

But not everything we tell ourselves is true. Records are about forgetting, via a process akin to appraisal. I mean, in this instance, records at the point of creation are designed to leave out information. Even as we write something down to remember it for the future, just at the point that we photograph a scene to recall its shapes at some later time, we are unconsciously forgetting. We create, in the form of records, rememberings that are also forgottenings. We turn our back to the ugly building falling apart to photograph a small purple crocus bursting from the mulch around the trunk of a tree. We decide to interview one person for an oral history, because we believe another cannot tell us what we need to know. When we create records, we create an edited version of the past.

This first degree of appraisal—the decision to create or not create a record—is one the record creator constantly faces. This initial step determines what the archivist will be able to appraise, because we usually appraise extant records.[2] Second degree appraisal is what archivists do: we assess the value of records that exist, records that survived long enough for us to find them. We are never the only appraisers. Creators of records are constantly destroying records we might identify as have enduring value. We don't even know how often it happens, though we usually tell stories of such intentional mishaps—or of the unintentional ones caused by disasters of various types.

Archivists hold themselves aloft with the sense that we are preservers of memory, that we develop systems to ensure our fellow humans can see back into a rich past—not just the past we all learn via the news, but a deeper understanding of the past, and of humanity's many accomplishments and failures within it. We see ourselves as members of a memory profession. We profess the value of memory.

But the best memory is often the forgotten one. There can sit, deep in a human mind, the moldering reminder of a terrible episode in one's life—one received at the hands of another, but also possibly one we have wrought upon someone else when acting through the worst versions of ourselves. Our worst selves we want no-one to know. Our worst pain we often hide from everyone, maybe even when we have shamed ourselves unfairly for something we did not even do. Maybe because it is simply too painful to remember.

As an example of remembering as a method of forgetting, I'll give you this example from my own life, my own experience with memory.

I have a long memory but an extremely shallow one. The earliest two memories I can recall are from when I was about two, and the earliest I can accurately date was from when I was just under two years old.[3] The first of my pair of memories was either my walking along the back of a couch before a large plate-glass window filled with sunlight (this is a story of climbing and balance and joy) or my crouching behind a trash can to hide from neighborhood children who were trying to beat me (a two-year-old) up.[4] The first of these I date as my earliest memory, but the proper sequencing of memories is usually difficult, though it is made easier for me because I have moved so often in my life. But the earliest recorded and datable memory of mine is of me breaking my nose (or having it broken for me).[5]

Note that these memories are from earlier in a life than the earliest memories most people retain. I believe the violence of the beginning of my life, often at the hands of equally young children, has helped me remember back so far. Even today, my dreams are usually dreams of escape from bands of people pursuing me with ill intent. I was a very shy child,[6] so other children believed—correctly, it turns out—that they could take advantage of me, wreak their childlike dominion over my body and self.

COURT OF CHANCERY DOCUMENTS EXHIBITING MOUSECHEW

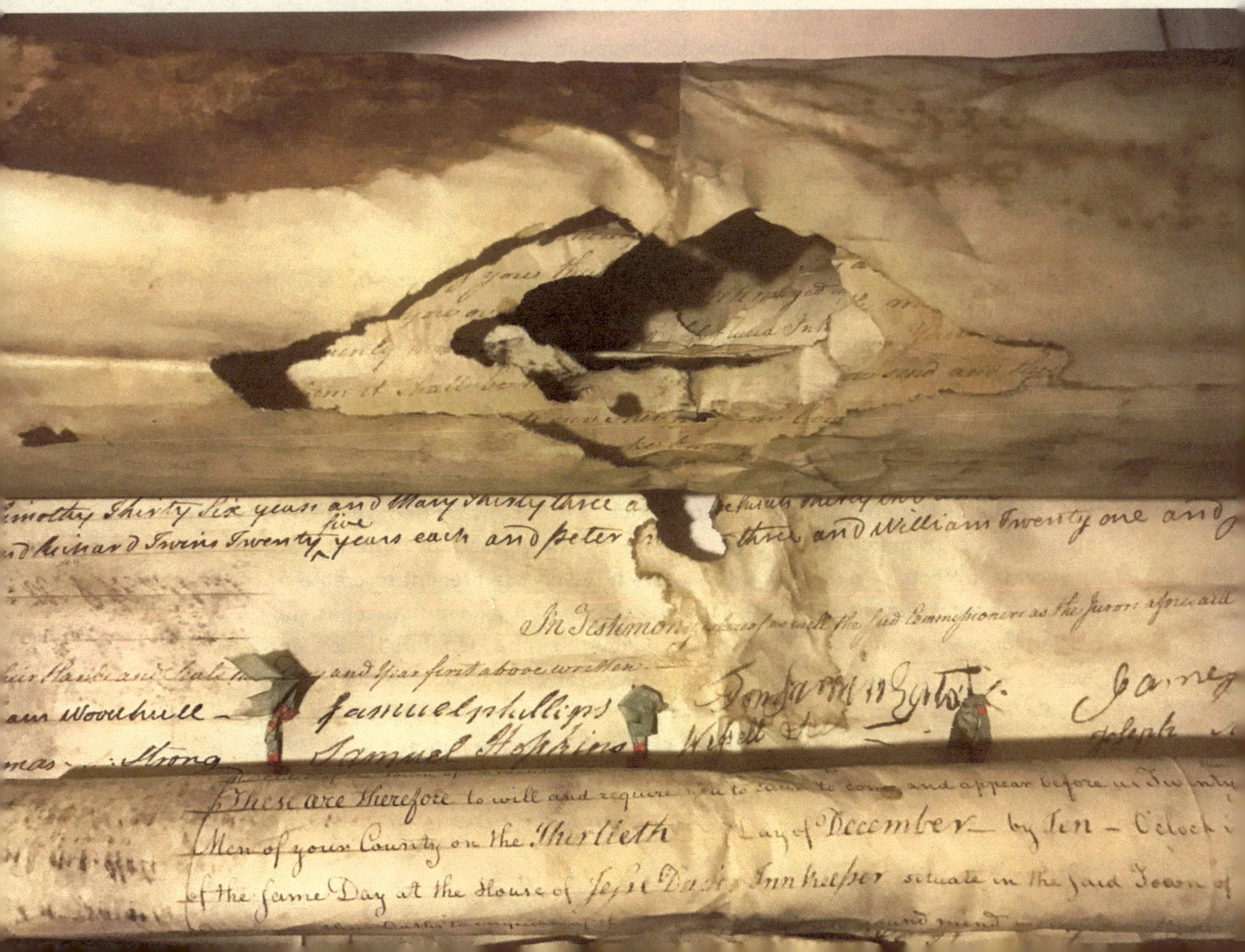

I have hundreds, thousands, of very specific memories. I remember the visual outlines of places extremely well. When I returned to my hometown of Porto, Portugal for the first time this year, I navigated to the locations of sites of importance to me in my old neighborhood via my 50-year-old memory of those spaces. When I was trying to locate the Palacio do Cristal in Porto, having forgotten its name, I found it while driving by and then recognizing the wall encircling that park.

Yet these memories are fragmentary and visual. If I run into a colleague I haven't seen in a decade, I will forget their name but I will remember very specific encounters with the person and be able to visualize exactly where we stood and what we discussed. But those memories are scattered and apparently remembered for random reasons or because they are somehow touchstones to my past, even if only vague representations of that past. I remember almost to the beginning of my childhood. I remember the traumas and joys of my life, but I forget and have forgotten much else.

I have come to conclude that I have intentionally forgotten most of my past, afraid of the details I might recall, because my childhood was quite violent. I never recall physical pain, though I remember when I should have experienced such. I also believe I inaccurately erase unwanted memories. I leave the most unforgettable of these intact even if submerged, no matter how traumatic they are, but I also forget essential information I need in my daily personal and professional life. Once, about fifteen years ago, I forgot a word and stomped my foot on the boards beneath my feet to bring attention to the concept I had temporarily forgotten the name of: *floor.* Which is to say that our memories, especially our own biologically stored ones, are always also a means by which we discard what we care not to recall any longer.

Records, just as minds, can also be havens for forgetting. The European concept of the right to be forgotten sets down in law a process to hide the shameful or private parts of individuals' pasts to allow people some comfort within the cocoon of collective forgetting. Once that hidden record is gone,[7] fewer people will learn of it. Once the last person remembering the event dies, there will be no record to remind us.

But intentional forgetting at the level of a society is not always benevolent, not always an act of mercy and charity. The most powerful acts of forgetting are governmental acts of overwriting the past and even the present to create an inaccurate view of a nation and its actions. In Burma,[8] the government has supported for years a series of lies to support the murder, rape, denaturalization, and expulsion of its Rohingya minority. They use various lies to bolster their falsehoods, the most important of which is to claim the Rohingya are not Burmese but actually Bangladeshi.[9] The government claims this Muslim minority in its Buddhist-majority country has only recently invaded Burma, even though the historical record demonstrates the Rohingya have lived there at least since 1799.[10] The Burmese government, partly in the form of Aung Sun Suu Kyi,[11] announced it would no longer use the term *Rohingya* in official documents,[12] because even recognizing a name is to recognize a people. So forgetting can be a process of pasting over facts with lies.

The Burmese are not at all alone in this. I provide this outline of the Burmese situation only as one example of a form of forgetting via recordkeeping and memorymaking. We could easily identify hundreds of other examples across the millennia, even the erasure of the poet Sappho from the written record, a task so successful we are left almost always with mere fragments of her words—usually saved only because they were quoted in other works, ones praising her poetry.

What forgetting consists of, in all these cases, is replacing a true memory with an imagined one (or a void). Certainly, all humans do this to some degree. It is a natural process of our brains to remember incorrectly, to recall what didn't happen, and to forget its analog, what actually did. The human mind is a poor recordkeeping system, because it is not inviolate. We forget details, we slough away most of the experiences we have had, and dementia eats away at the remaining memories of some of us, while sometimes also revealing memories we have forgotten. The historical record, if managed well, is stable and unchanging, reliable and sure. What is said within it may be false, but our proper care of it can ensure it doesn't become something different than it originally was. We are not caretakers of truths but of records.

We will always forget—by what we intentionally leave out of the record, by what records we destroy, and by how soon we destroy them. And we like it this way. We are reasonable people who live in the real world. We cannot remember the entire past. To wish for that is too quixotic for a sensible people. We want the solace of remembering what we find worth remembering. We enjoy stripping away the unnecessary static in our lives so we can thrive with a manageable volume of memories.

We don't want to remember too much.

Photographs, because of their transparency and truth, were thus credited with being not only a way of seeing across space, but also a way of seeing those things—qualities, characteristics, emotions, values—that, in space, had no observable manifestation.

Joan Schwartz, "'Records of Simple Truth and Precision': Photography, Archives, and the Illusion of Control," *Archivaria* 50 (2000): 16.

#archivesquotes #truth

The Content of Context

The content of a record consists of the information shown to us; content is what the record says. The context of that same record consists of the overlying systems of connection, knowledge, and fact that help us understand what the record means.

We archivists often exclaim such sentences as "Context is very important to archivists," but we usually see context through a narrow lens that restricts the true breadth of contextuality. We, if possibly unconsciously, treat context in terms of what I call structural context and we imagine context to be innate to the process of the record's creation—when the latter is only occasionally the case.

Let me note here, that I don't see structure as part of a tripartite system of the basic attributes of a record. Instead, I see structure as just another form of context, that form most innate to the record itself. To me, content and context are two pieces that fit together to form a whole, to allow for the transmission of authentic knowledge. They represent the yin and yang of archives.

Structural context, in my contextual schema, concerns how records and records series are internally organized and how different records series interacted with one another during active use, so this type of context has both micro and macro incarnations.

At the granular level, structural context is truly textual—though also visual and possibly numerical. The structure of a document explains how it works, calcifies how it is meant to mean. Headings and subheadings, internal hyperlinks, color, and even paragraphing structure a record and allow us to understand it. (If this does not make sense to you, imagine you were reading the Latin of the early Romans, in which they sometimes did not even allow spaces to interrupt the flow of text. Structure supports meaning; chaos and lack of structure decrease it.)

But structural context also exists in a less palpable way at the level of the series and at what I call the supraseries. The concept of a records series we are well familiar with; it is a set of records held together by purpose, record type, or method of filing. The series usually supports a particular function or a distinct part of a function. The supraseries is a collection of series that supports the same function, often a broad general function. In the context of early New York courts, the function of managing a civil court case necessitated the creation of various series: pleadings, writs, bail pieces, rules (later known as orders), affidavits, calendars, minutes, judgments, and satisfactions pieces—to name a few in roughly the order they would occur in an individual civil case. When we treat these series as components of a supraseries, we help clarify this structural context for users, who otherwise might not realize that context.

Which takes us to the most important concept we need to remember about context: we must document it. Whether a record's context is obvious to us or not, it might not be to others in the future, so our finding aids must be less focused on finding and more focused on knowing. We can dispense with detailed folder lists to make time to indicate the interconnections between series. People need to find records, but their greatest need is to know them, to understand how they work.

I call this documentation of context "contextualization," because it is the active process of collecting information about context, information which—even if native to the record—is often unspoken, almost invisible, and sometimes only knowable by the process of research or relatively deep interaction with a body of records.

Contextualization is the process of understanding complex sets of records by investigating and documenting their complex (and ever-growing) webs of connection. In this conceptualization, records are always made more knowable by understanding them through the many contexts they operate within. The creation of context does not end when the records are no longer being created and the creators have vanished. Instead, context continues to grow as secondary data on the records continues to be created by archivists and by those writing about the records and their creators—and even by those using the records. Some of this information is technically granular metadata, but some of it is merely the creation and documentation of insights into the records by explaining the history of the records and their creators. These contexts are both internal and external to their creating organizations and synchronous and asynchronous with the same.

The possible types of context are nearly limitless—in the same way types of value are within archivy, but over the course of my work with archives I have identified a few basic types of context, though I can think of many others

Historical context is one of the most easily understood forms, the one we tend to address, at least in part, through administrative histories and biographical notes. Such historical notes must record the basic relevant context for users. What is most important, though, is to document the individual histories of the records' creators, which are usually harder to assemble than already well know general historical facts.

Functional context provides information on the specific and distinct functions of each creating unit and on how these operated. In a true archival fonds, this functional context materializes in the form of a rich and interconnected information ecosystem, though also one that changes over time. Understanding the interrelations between the functions within a single unit and the broader interrelations between the other units at varying levels in the hierarchy allows a potential user to better understand the functions of these bodies and how those functions once guided the world of those units.

Procedural context focuses on the specific actions a unit conducted to support a single function, and this context is usually demonstrated at the level of the series description. This context helps users understand how units operated at their granular level so that they can conceptualize and understand those procedures and thus understand how the records worked in practice.

Physical context is a tricky one, because it can easily mislead us. For instance, two volumes found next to each other on a shelf may merely indicate that unlike records have been thrown together during a time when records were in disarray. However, physical propinquity is often a significant fact indicating a set of records fits together as a whole. Determining the organic bond between a body of records kept naturally together helps make those records more knowable: having more examples of records in one place and realizing they serve the same function helps us determine what they are about.

The concept of human context accepts that knowing the specific individuals who carried out certain tasks can help users identify and understand the records better. For instance, the pleadings submitted to the New York Supreme Court of Judicature were written by the attorneys themselves, so the focus of an individual attorney's work would imbue such documents with additional significance just as much as the attorney's unique handwriting did. An interesting example of human context is how specific people's signatures on documents or in record volumes can help archivists identify the creator and series of a vagrant record.

Custodianship is neither static nor constant, so information on custodial context will change with time. Important to understanding this type of context is information about how the original custodians of records kept, managed, and arranged or re-arranged the records. But custodial context does not end with the original custodians, because archival records have multiple custodians who share responsibility across a chain of time. Later custodians may alter the arrangement of the records, apply different metadata to the records, and otherwise reconceptualize the original custodian's original management of the records—all of which the archivist should document to show how and when thinking about the records changed. However, physical distance is also context and may indicate records physically apart from each other do not form a series. Physical context is primarily of importance to the archivist (rather than the user), who will use it to restore the intended order of the records.

There exists, in my conceptualization, a context I call the context of record dispersal, which is important in at least three ways. First, this context explains how related records (even records from the same series) were dispersed to other repositories or persons. This dispersal is important to codify because it will tell a user where they must go, beyond the central repository or source, to find and use the records. This context conceptually reassembles the series. Second, this type of context explains how records maintained in the same storage area or working environment became dispersed and disarranged over time. Third, the context of records dispersal must address the inexplicable absence of records and note the degree of that absence. Some records have been lost over time, and it is important for future users to know this, for them to know what is missing, even if the absolute knowledge of loss eliminates the hope of ever finding a record.

In the concept of the context of multiplicities, information is rarely imagined to be unique within an interconnected recordkeeping system. Usually, there existed built-in duplication, even during the age of the scribe. Early New York courts, for instance, often produced two sets of minutes: a draft set of minutes called rough minutes, and a finished set called engrossed minutes. The latter were the better source, but absent those the rough minutes could answer questions and support work functions. In the context of multiplicities, we document what these multiples were and how they differed from each other. Once the world entered the era of relatively easy reproduction, the means of multiplication expanded in many ways, via faxing, spirit duplicating, photocopying, microfilming, digitization, or laser-printing—thus producing varyingly authentic and reliable records.

Metadata has become a central focus of archivy in our time, but the context of metadata vis-à-vis the records themselves is not always deeply appreciated. Even in controlled environments, metadata isn't static. It changes because of changing standards, internal needs, and staff. Because of the importance of metadata to the use of records, archivists must do more than create metadata. They also have to explain earlier metadata and define how the metadata function—or fail to function—as intended.

Although paradata is not a concept common to the world of archives, paradata context is important in a world focused on information. Paradata, simply, explains metadata and how it was created. Archivists must create and document paradata (data about data about data) whenever they create metadata, and sometimes they will have to reverse engineer and explicate unrecorded paradata employed by custodians before them. Certainly, I have had to.

My concept of literary context might be the most vaporous of contexts. As I have said, I believe context grows over time. This happens as humans create new texts and develop new ideas out of the records themselves, causing the pull of the records on the human thought to grow over time. Every book or article that has used such records, every recorded presentation or exhibition that presented these records and put them in new contexts adds to literary context. Literary context may seem synonymous with historical context, but the latter is the pure recording—impossible as it is to do—of what actually happened. Literary context concerns the ways in which the recorded idea is used to extend the context of the record beyond the purely historical, to tie the records into ideas never before conceived.

Context is neither simple nor stable. An unchanging record changes over time because the way we see it does. And the reason for that is the second most basic concept in archives: context.

The most basic, of course, is content.

COURT OF CHANCERY EXHIBIT, FRAGMENT OF THE ACCOUNT BOOK OF HALLETT AND WOODWARD (1774–1775)

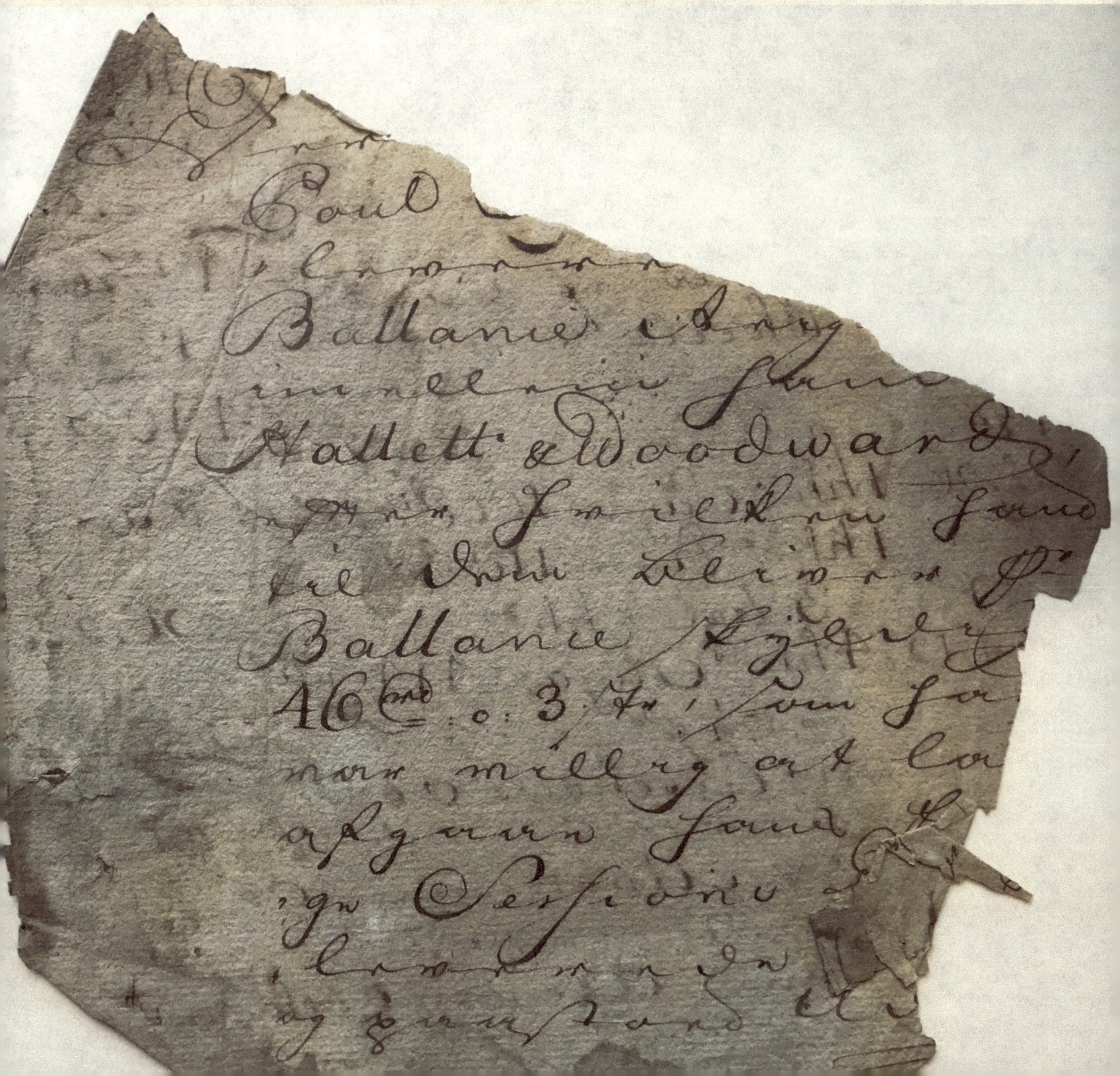

I am much more than an archivist, I am a connection to their past.

Steven D. Booth (quoted by Michelle Novak, @michnovak, Twitter) in "How Can I Help? Providing Exceptional Service and Practicing the Ethics of Care in the Archives" (Society of American Archivists Conference: Austin, Texas, 6 August 2019).

#archivesquotes #SAA19 #S904

To Preserve the Record, Protect the Three M's

The basic concepts we accept without question are often the most difficult to pin down. The world which appears so clear to us in our unconsidered thoughts becomes contradictory and indeterminate when we begin to think about it closely. So it is with preservation.

We might begin our considerations here by wondering what *preservation* means. Does it refer to any actions we take to ensure something (in our case, archives) remains viable and usable, or does it mean the state that records are in because of (or despite or regardless of the absence of) such actions? Certainly, it means both. Then why does our language not distinguish between our actions and the related circumstances of the record? It cannot be because our grasp of how to preserve records has been so sure. We have spent centuries employing preservation strategies that reduced the viability of records. Even now, when preservation procedures are based on empirical studies, we continue to stumble into error—yet records also continue to persist despite our imperfect practices.

If a paper record remains whole but slowly yellows over time, does it exhibit a state of preservation or a fluid state moving from preservation to eventual disintegration?

Let's assume, for simplicity's sake, that the act of preservation means the practice of caring for records, to whatever degree is practical, in a manner that reduces the chances of the destruction or the slow degradation of records. This means wealthier organizations will have better preservation programs and will be able to preserve records for longer periods of time, but it also means preservation will come to an end for every record at some point in the future, when the molecules in the record simply can no longer cohere. Let's also say that a state of preservation is one in which the records remain largely knowable even when their carrier medium is seriously degraded.

But this definition assumes preservation means the preservation of the original carrier medium. If the medium persists, then the records exist. This is a dictum so central to our profession that no-one mentions it. As most dicta, it is only partially true. Across the millennia, preservation has also been achieved by transferring the information in a record from one medium to another.

In the wide era before the onset of printing, manuscripts were copied onto new pages both to create new copies and to revive an overused copy before it fell into total dissolution. The transfer of information from paper to paper or parchment to parchment helped preserve the information—in part because lots of copies kept stuff safe centuries before we acronymized that concept.[1] We extended this concept of replacement as preservation with the implementation of microfilm. A basic point of microfilming was always to reduce the quantity of physical space records inhabit, but it was also used as a preservation tool. An archives might microfilm a most treasured set of records, retain those in their original form, and require users to access the information via the resulting film. They might also keep a master copy of the microfilm far off site to ensure they had a safely distant backup of the records. Or the archives could even replace the paper records with the microfilm itself, thus producing a form of preservation where the original was discarded in place of the more durable copy.

That plan often ran into problems. Microfilm is high-grain photographic film, so it can capture detail exquisitely, so long as you microfilm expertly and all the detail required can be captured in black and white without significant loss of information. Even if both these were true, users often faced[2] microfilm readers of such low quality that interpreting a clear image of a faded document on a fuzzy microfilm screen reduced access to the information because it slowed down the ability of the person to read the text. This scenario does not even raise the issue that moving the length of a reel forward at a brisk clip—the machine whirring and hissing as it went—left many users (including me) nauseated by the time they arrived at the frame they had been in search of. Still, it is difficult to argue against microfilm as a preservation medium. If it is polyester-based,[3] it is generally rated as having a life expectancy of 500 years, and storing microfilm in the proper environment is relatively inexpensive.

Preservation isn't clear cut. We don't always know if we have achieved it, or if we can maintain it.

With the acceptance of digitization as a preservation methodology, we have begun to expand our concept of preservation. However, many people still do not accept digitization as a preservation solution, because the preservation of digital materials (the resulting images, in this case) is more difficult than for hardcopy ones. Formats change, digital records standards change, and being digital means constantly renovating our data management systems: updating hardware

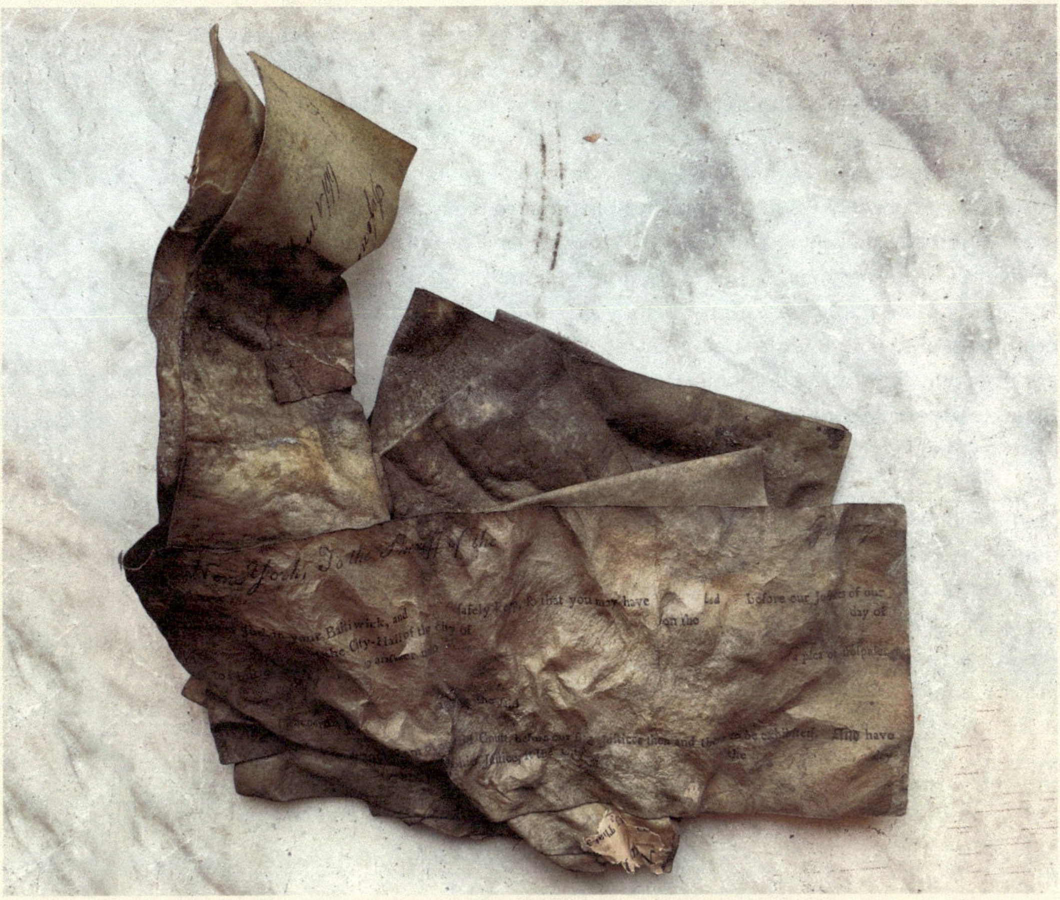

HEAT-DAMAGED PARCHMENT WRITS OF THE NEW YORK SUPREME COURT OF JUDICATURE (1799)

and software, migrating files occasionally to new file formats, even tearing down one system to replace it in toto with another. Preservation aims for stability, but its processes aren't stable; they must change as needs and technology change.

Digitization, however, brings with it a deeper incarnation of what replacement preservation is. When we microfilm a document and dispose of the paper, we are left with a black and clear image on a piece of polyester. We have not captured the document in all its details: not its color, not the grain of the paper, not its feel nor its scent.[4] Although microfilm is fine grained, digitization can capture nearly infinitely finer detail and also capture color, thus providing something closer to the aura of the original document—which look and feel is often lost when the document is reduced to black and white. The digital provides a copy we can zoom in on to see the details of the paper and the letters upon it. The digital more accurately represents the record's first or earliest captured state.

With the huge stores of distressed and disintegrating paper records archives still hold, we will likely succumb to digitization to preserve many of them. Only the other day, I found a handful of bail pieces from the first half of the 1800s, some so black with an old dry mold their faces folded in place were nearly unreadable. One preservation solution would be to humidify, unfold, and flatten these papers; and carefully wash each of the brittle sheets in a water wash and dry them. But the mold will persist, even if at low levels. Even professional attempts to kill mold with ethylene oxide or gamma radiation may not entirely succeed. The best option might be to ensure they are readable and then digitize them, print them onto stable rag paper, integrate those copies with the rest of the paper files, and destroy the originals. Or the best option might merely be to destroy them, to accept they have some value but not enough to require us to take steps to save them.

Thinking in terms of preservation is often a mistake for archivists. We must abandon some records. We must be practical even when we are always idealistic. We must remember that striving towards perfection is striving towards disaster.

We accept without even a second's thought that preservation means preserving the core information in the record, which information I call the message in this context. If we lose the message, we lose everything. But we also need to preserve the medium, be it paper, parchment, film, or even whatever media we

NEW YORK CORONER'S INQUEST OF MARGARET BARBERY DAGBREIN (30 DECEMBER 1762)

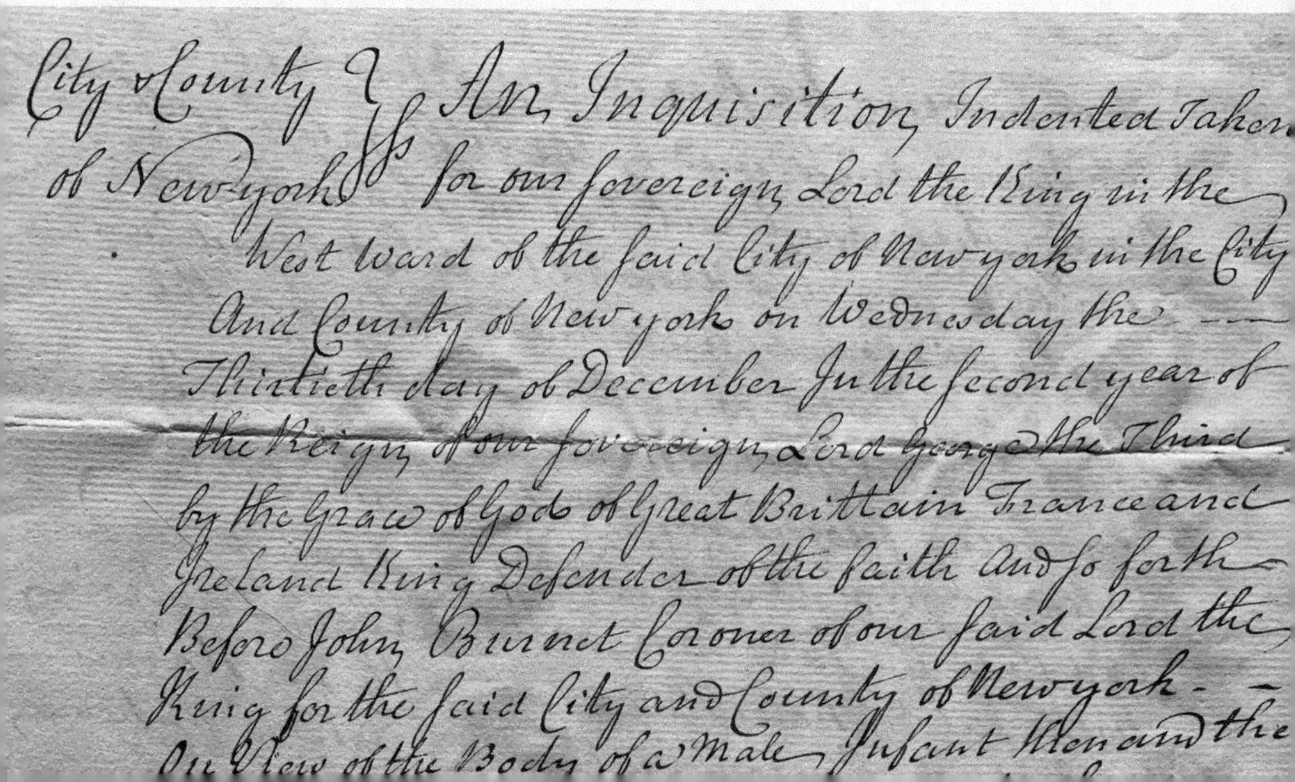
City & County } ss An Inquisition Indented Taken
of New-york } for our Sovereign Lord the King in the
West ward of the said City of New york in the City
And County of New york on Wednesday the
Thirtieth day of December In the second year of
the Reign of our Sovereign Lord George the Third
by the Grace of God of Great Brittain France and
Ireland King Defender of the faith And so forth
Before John Burnet Coroner of our said Lord the
King for the said City and County of New york
On View of the Body of a Male Infant then and there

might use to store bytes. The format of the message and the medium itself might change, but we must protect both to preserve the record. The medium can lose the message and still exist, pointless as that would be for us, but the message cannot exist without a carrier—it must exist somewhere in space.[5]

Yet there is a third M that we must preserve to ensure we have saved a knowable record.[6] Knowability is most important. I have found scraps of records that make no sense out of the context of any other records. And records found still whole might themselves be meaningless without clarifying context. To truly preserve a record, we must have enough contextual metadata to allow us to understand how the record functioned and what it was originally communicating. Obsolete arcane work processes, missing inherent metadata, and the absence of relational context can easily conspire to make a record nearly worthless from a data point of view.

Metadata, however, is not one simple thing. Instead, it[7] is various things. In my thinking, metadata comes in two basic different forms: inherent and constructed.[8]

To be sure, both kinds of metadata are constructed, but inherent metadata is native to the record. If you have a wordprocessing document with a filename and automatically recorded metadata, such as the creator's name, the date of creation, and even the wordcount; if you have a digital photograph that records the geographical coordinates of its creation, its size in megabytes, and the f-stop employed—all those metadata are inherent to the record. Even in a paper context, records bear inherent metadata. Minute books carry the dates and locations of meetings, page numbers, headings identifying major topics discussed, and even the secretary's name. This metadata can also be lost, even if the record partially survives.

About twenty years ago, I visited the Town of Jay's office in the Adirondacks of New York as part of my work as a regional advisory officer for the New York State Archives. As with many rural local governments, the town had stored its older records—what we might call its archives—in the town barn. At least one box of records was stored on the bare earth of the barn. Over time, moisture from the ground moved via capillary action into the town's earliest volume of minutes, and the volume had rested in that place for so long that about one third of it had worn away. Fraying moist flaps of paper, covered in green and purple mold, reached out of the core of the volume. When we examined the book, we realized it had been resting on the earth head downward, allowing the biological process of decay to eat through the top part of the book, meaning that all the important metadata had disappeared: dates, location, names of people in attendance, and maybe the time of the meetings. This volume from the 1800s, a rarity in the Adirondacks, was undatable, and most people's names were gone, thus removing a possible means of roughly dating the entries. The record could no longer function as an authentic record; it had ceased to be sufficiently knowable. The record—in a real sense, and not just the missing third of it—had been lost. Preservation was impossible because knowability had disappeared.

Constructed metadata comes later, because it is metadata not native to the record itself. Archivists create constructed metadata to do one of two things: to ensure or increase the knowability of a record. I believe archivists often create more metadata needed and create granular metadata more frequently and with greater vigor than they do collective metadata. Sometimes, we must create metadata to make records more accessible for users, and that is what granular metadata does. For instance, I created a system of granular and inherent metadata (the names of people, actions, locations, and dates). What we do a little less is build systems of collective metadata that put bodies of records in context with other bodies of records so users can understand them better.

In my work, I have virtually eschewed granular metadata, except in the case of the occasional folder title. My focus has been on collective metadata, which provides information on sets of records. Ancient court records and the processes that cause their creation are often inscrutable to people new to them, so I developed tools to help people understand the processes. Sometimes, the tool might be merely a note in a series description explaining the sequence of steps in a legal process, thus giving the user a way to determine which document would have come first and which would be the response to it. Other tools included a glossary to explain the meaning of old legal terms, especially those in Latin and the few symbolic abbreviations. (What I could not provide was a guide to reading secretary hand, though I addressed that issue by noting in the series description the writing system used—to help the user find a tool to help them decipher the script.) I created a thirty-six-page document on writs, which explained the categories of writs, each individual type of writ and its purpose, provided illustrations of each type (since different writs took different shapes), and I included a visual guide that located and explained the identifying information (let's say, metadata) found on the front of writs. I also created regnal calendars, so users could quickly identify the year of a document occurring in March during the second year of the reign of George III. Unexpectedly, I had to produce one such calendar for years of independence, since the courts of New York identified the year of a document by the year of the country's independence for nearly fifty years.

I focus on collective metadata, which is more difficult and time-consuming to produce, because it helps preserve records by preserving—or at least presenting—the various contexts in which those records operated. And I do this for another, related, reason:

Granular metadata makes records findable. Collective metadata makes them knowable.

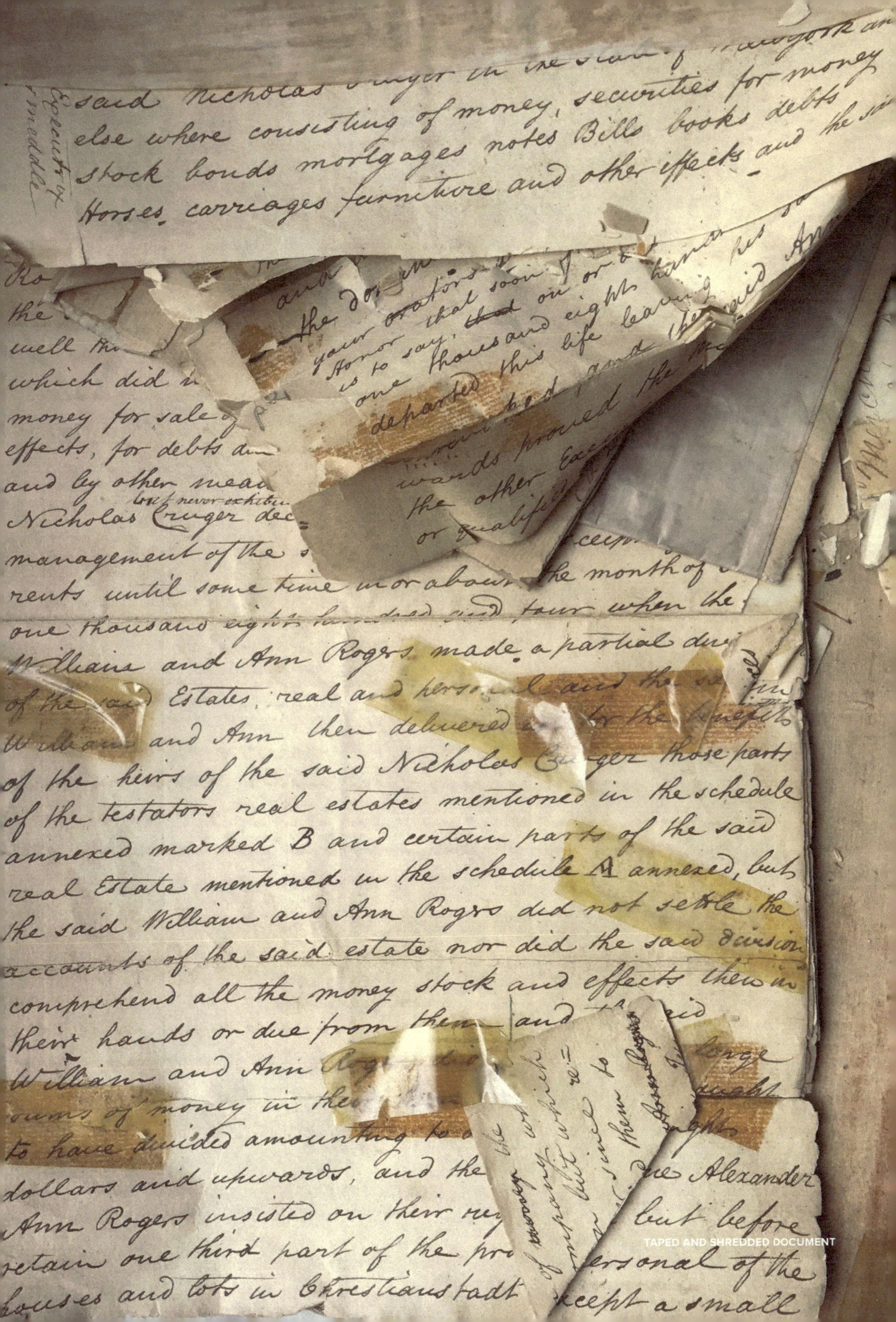

said Nicholas Cruger in the state of New York an[d]
else where consisting of money, securities for money
stock bonds mortgages notes Bills books debts
Horses, carriages furniture and other effects and the s[illegible]

[illegible] your orators [illegible]
Honor that soon [illegible]
is to say that on or [illegible]
one thousand eight hundred [illegible]
departed this life leaving his [illegible]
[illegible] wards proved and the said Ann [illegible]
the other Exec[illegible]
or qualified [illegible]

the [illegible]
well th[illegible]
which did [illegible]
money for sale of [illegible]
effects, for debts an[illegible]
and by other mea[illegible]
Nicholas Cruger dec[illegible]
management of the [illegible] receiv[illegible]
rents until some time in or about the month of [illegible]
one thousand eight hundred and four when the
William and Ann Rogers made a partial div[illegible]
of the said Estates, real and personal and the sa[illegible]
William and Ann then delivered over for the benefit
of the heirs of the said Nicholas Cruger those parts
of the testators real estates mentioned in the schedule
annexed marked B and certain parts of the said
real Estate mentioned in the schedule A annexed, but
the said William and Ann Rogers did not settle the
accounts of the said estate nor did the said division
comprehend all the money stock and effects then in
their hands or due from them and the said
William and Ann Rog[illegible] large
sums of money in the[illegible] ought
to have divided amounting to [illegible]
dollars and upwards, and the [illegible] the Alexander
Ann Rogers insisted on their [illegible] but before
retain one third part of the pro[illegible] personal of the
houses and lots in Christiansted [illegible] except a small

TAPED AND SHREDDED DOCUMENT

A record is an evolving mediation of understanding about some phenomenon—a mediation created by social and technical processes of inscription, transmission, and contextualization.

Tom Nesmith, "Still Fuzzy, But More Accurate: Some Thoughts on the 'Ghosts' of Archival Theory," *Archivaria* 47 (1999): 145.

#archivesquotes #context

Record as Organism, Records as Ecosystem

An example of a more complex information system would be a system to collect and store data to support the evaluation of teachers, schools, and school districts across a state. This system could have thousands of separate institutions accumulating and supplying data according to precise standards, it could consist of dozens or scores of separable modules that share some information between modules but not all, and it could be used to evaluate the performance of individual teachers, students, administrators, or schools. Such a system is not just a beast of technology; it is also a political mechanism, an informational construct that reveals the interest in public education at a certain point in time, a bureaucratic system informed as much by the rules for its creation as it is by the information so created, and it is a multi-dimensional and multi-organizational system maintained, by hundreds of thousands of people, as an immense integrated ecosystem of informational ecosystems. The level of complexity here is one that cannot even be fathomed by the archivist without careful analysis of the system of rules, the structure, and the actual implementation of these. A system like this one changes the rules of appraisal.

The opening paragraph above was edited out of a book (well, a module of a book) I wrote on appraising digital records.[1] The editor silently removed this paragraph in his first pass over the manuscript, which excision I could accept—though I still wanted to give readers a sense of how complex an information ecosystem could actually be, and how difficult a job we would have to understand, appraise, adequately contextualize, and care for records in such a system. The example I give of a system is not even a product of my imagination. It was, instead, a distilled description of an information system I had appraised in the then recent past.[2]

The system I described was not part of an imagined future, but integral to our continuing present. The information age is the age of the archivist (and the information technologist and the digital asset manager and other kin), and the archivist will be continually challenged to address the needs and difficulties of our information era. What interests me here is how the records environments we encounter will become increasingly rich and, thus, increasingly complex. Because these systems are organic environments, we will need to replicate or describe these to provide users the context needed to understand how records operated within them.

A record is one small participant in an informational ecosystem, one that moves and changes over time. We prefer to believe in the ineluctable stability of the record—it is stored here, it means this, it is connected to this process—but the record changes as its environment changes, even as the contents of the record itself remains inviolate. At the simplest level, a record in a digital ecosystem may always be stored in one set conceptual location—leaving aside that fact that there will usually be copies of it held in various physical locations to ensure its survival. However, the conceptual location of a record may also change over time. Sometimes, people merge projects and decide to transfer documents from one folder to another; webmasters often modify the structure of a website (or its system of URLs) without changing the information within it.

Most importantly, as records proliferate around any record, the context and significance of the record change and increase. The record begins to mean something different and operate differently in a more robust environment. As context diversifies and expands, features of the record not previously noticed become prominent. The records are transformed, yet left physically unchanged, by their interaction with other records within their native environment.

A single record is an organism within its ecosystem. When it first is born, its value may be greater because it is unique and singular, or it may be lesser because it is isolated and unitary. Usually, its meaning expands with time, as new records are introduced into this world and as other records are created, in part, out of the information in that first document—thus spreading its informational DNA into the ecosystem and ensuring the survival of the message. This genetic concept of records derives from the notion of archival ramification promoted by Shirley Carvalhêdo Franco. She encapsulates her thinking about ramification (and its ramifications) in this sentence of hers:

> The existence of ramification confirms the argument, therefore, that the complete and absolute destruction of all archives related to a specific historical event would be practically impossible: archival documents tend to "escape" attempts of total destruction, becoming almost immune to complete elimination.[3]

What she is telling us here is that in any rich and interconnected information environment, in any complex fonds, data is replicated and dispersed. The same document is stored within different series or held by more than one department. Essential information within one file is echoed in scores of other documents, as the central data of the organization are processed and shared within and without the organization. This process mirrors the distribution of DNA within a natural environment. Biological organisms reproduce, thus mixing and distributing their DNA. Some of these organisms migrate from their home ecosystem into new environments and set up new colonies supporting and distributing their shared DNA, the equivalent of collective memory in an archives conceptualization. The organisms are eventually replaced by their offspring as most older records are discarded. These newer documents added to the series ensure the series persists even as older records within it are lost or destroyed. Even over the course of millennia, an organism might carry genetic markers of its earliest ancestors—thus a person (an information-bearing object of a different kind) can be identified by his maternal haplogroup H4a1 and his paternal haplogroup R-L51.[4]

The replication of human or record DNA allows evidence of the past to continue even after the death or destruction of most of the DNA of an interrelated set of organisms, whether they be data or biological ones. The power of the undiminished fonds is that it allows for discrete and unique bits of information in concert with robust repetition and the replication of essential information, which gives the fonds the ability to survive some degree of data loss yet continue to transfer information into the future. In the same way, a biological ecosystem can survive catastrophe well enough to replace the flora and fauna eradicated in a volcanic eruption or a tidal wave, even while losing some genetic information.

Archivists often refer to records systems as organic because we recognize the truth of these points I have been making. We understand these systems are as bountiful, self-replicating, and interdependent as any robust biological ecosystem. What this also means is not every records system is healthy. Many have suffered debilitating information losses so severe they cannot reproduce themselves and they cannot protect essential data within their bare branches. The causes of such diminishment are many, but they actually include someone dear to our personal considerations: the archivist—or at least the archivist manqué.

And this is how we move into a new environment—not a natural one, not the native environment of any record, but the constructed environment, the faux environment, the unnatural environment, something I might call the archival zoo. In a zoological park, there is limited integration of subsidiary parts of the ecosystem into the whole, and with good reason: the animals displayed for us originated in vastly different environments: the arctic, the savannah, the isthmic jungle, the ocean. The variety of creatures cannot share a single sub-ecosystem, so their environments must take the form of an archipelago of isolated island ecosystems. Also, the zookeepers cannot allow the lions to kill and eat all the antelope. The ecosystem of a zoo is too small to allow the natural order of the veldt to replicate itself. This unnatural environment is too weak, too biologically narrow and shallow, to allow for natural replication under natural conditions.

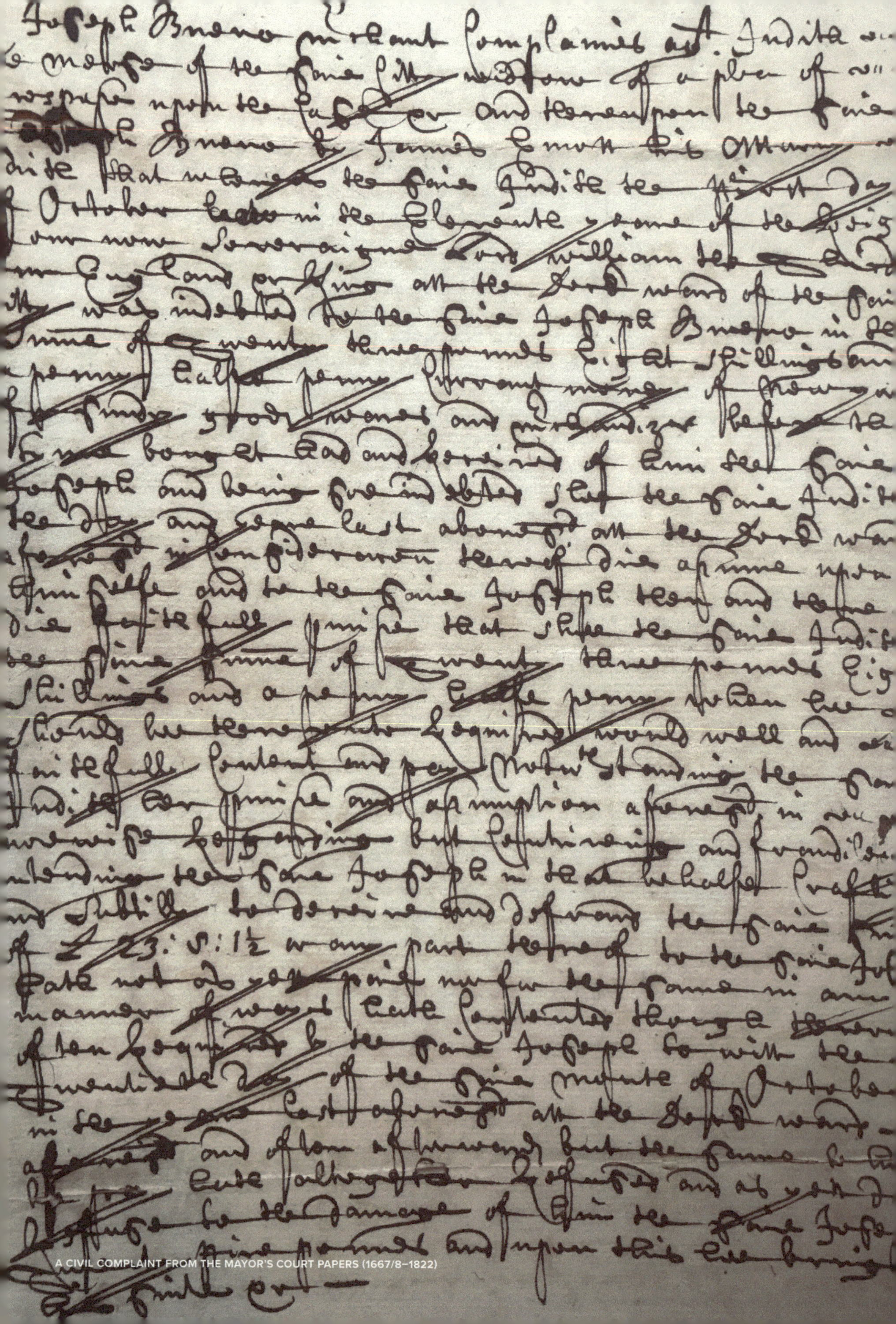

Joseph Bueno Plaintiff Complaines agt. Judith ... of a plea of trespass upon the case ... And thereupon the said Joseph Bueno by James Emott his Attorney saith that whereas the said Judith the first day of October in the Eleventh yeare of the Reigne of our now Soveraigne Lord William the Third ... of England &c King att the City of New York ... was indebted to the said Joseph Bueno in the summe of twenty three pounds Eight shillings and a penny halfe penny Currant money ... for divers goods wares and merchandize before that time bought had and received of him the said Joseph and being soe indebted shee the said Judith the day and yeare last abovesaid att the City of New York ... in consideracon thereof did assume upon her selfe and to the said Joseph then and there did faithfully promise that shee the said Judith the summe of twenty three pounds Eight Shillings and a penny halfe penny when shee should be thereunto required would well and faithfully Content and pay Notwithstanding the said Judith her promise and assumption aforesaid in noe wise regarding but Contriveing and fraudulently intending the said Joseph in that behalfe Craftily and Subtilly to deceive and defraud the said ... of £23: 8: 1½ or any part thereof to the said Joseph hath not as yet paid nor the same in any manner ... Contented though often required by the said Joseph ... the twentieth day of the same month of October in the yeare last aforesaid att the City of New York ... and often afterwards but the same to him ... hath altogether refused and as yet refuseth to the damage of him the said Joseph ... five pounds And upon this hee bringeth suite &c.

A CIVIL COMPLAINT FROM THE MAYOR'S COURT PAPERS (1667/8–1822)

The archival zoo consists of similar archival islands of genetic data, with one distinction from the zoo: in this case, records from various environments have been unnaturally mixed, rather than kept unnaturally separate from each other. Usually, we call such zoological agglomerations artificial collections, but they can take various related forms. In my own archives work, they take the forms of the artificial series and what I might call those of the fragmented and fused fonds. All of these are creations of the archivist as re-organizer. These practices originally derived from the library-focused historical manuscripts tradition in the United States,[5] and they demonstrate the librarianization[6] of archives—which, in this case, is based on the desire to organize information for efficient retrieval at the expense of protecting the natural order of records. This process is the process of merging into one somewhat like records that were never directly associated with each other.

The common example of this—which is quite manuscripts focused—is to create a collection[7] of historical correspondence relating to one topic and giving the entire created thing a title to hold it together. In this conception, the archivist manqué is pulling together papers that resemble each other along one axis but which are not naturally related, because they did not originate in the same native environment. Sometimes, these collections hold individual documents brought together to keep the curator from having to identify each document as a single, nearly vacant series. At other times, small batches of documents actually preserve a tiny corner of a now dispersed and impoverished documental ecosystem.

My personal world of archives encompasses most of the early courts of New York based near the bottom of the island of Manhattan.[8] The records traverse the 17th through the 21st centuries, and the earliest of these have often suffered through severe reorganizations. One example of an artificial series I have dealt with is the series I entitled "Court Papers, 1754–1837" of the Supreme Court of Judicature, which I found bearing the title "Pleadings on Parchment, 1754–1837." Ostensibly, this series was the earlier portion of the series, "Pleadings, 1837–1847,"[9] but a nosegay of problems makes such a conclusion impossible to assert. First, probably more than 50% of the soi-disant pleadings on parchment are on paper, thus undermining the entire point of treating this as a separate series (based, quizzically, on media format) and of identifying it as being on parchment. Yet other issues proliferate: The later pleadings truly are pleadings: papers submitted to the court by opposing sides in a civil dispute to plead their respective sides of a case.

The earlier pleadings do include such documents, which encompass a plethora of document types,[10] but they also include verdicts, various types of writs, jury panels, bail pieces—almost any document type that would be in any way related to a civil case. The records in the later series represent cases in the Supreme

Court of Judicature; those in the earlier series include records of that court but also of the Court of Chancery (a civil court, but one of equity), as well as the Court of General Sessions and the Court of Oyer and Terminer (the latter two being criminal courts, which have no connection to pleadings at all). So why were these records shoved together to form this series?[11] I assume the primary reason for this decision was to eliminate the need to segregate these records back into natural series.

Another series—"Writs, 1800–1910" of the Supreme Court—is the result of amalgamating multiple separate series of writs into one. Early inventories show that five sets of writs of the New York (County) Supreme Court existed as of the mid-1920s, and mid-century custodians merged all five together into an alphanumeric sequence that included writs of various other courts, including the Court of General Sessions, the Court of Oyer and Terminer, the New York Marine Court, and various district and police courts in New York City. The reason for this comingling was to create a single set of writs, to fashion an artificial alphanumeric arrangement scheme, and to index the writs so that patrons looking for writs could find them quickly.

The question is, Who looks for writs? Who looks for a particular document type? Users look for information. They have no concern what form that information takes. If this solution were truly user-based, why didn't these custodians merge all document types into case files? which would truly have provided users with the solution they would most desire—and which solution the courts themselves had implemented in 1910, so that possibility was already lying in plain view before them. In the end, I will transfer all the records from this series to different repositories that have a natural interest in adding these records to their own existing suprafonds of these courts' records—so I have already separated from this series, one by one, every record of the Supreme Court of Judicature until its 1847 reorganization. In this way, I have created my own pair of artificial series, though ones based on the intended order[12] (or, at least, the intended segregation) of the series.

What I deal with is a fragmented and fused fonds. In some cases, records have been dispersed from the core of their series, and I have done what is possible to return the records to their intended order. Sometimes, I faced boxes of documents of various types and entirely askew and had to create a sensible order I knew was not natural to the records. These are examples of fragmentation in the fonds, but these records also suffered the malady of fusion, which bothers my archival sense of decorum more. These occasionally huge series (a couple over 1,000 cubic feet in extent) were created by the interleaving of multiple records series from multiple courts.

These series intermix not just various series of one court, thus disrupting the intended order of those series. They also muddle the central provenance of the records, thus creating the illusion that the New York Supreme Court, the New York Superior Court, and the Court of Chancery were a single entity—rather than a collection of interrelated courts with different responsibilities and jurisdictions. We can never make right fragmented and fused fonds, especially one of this size.[13] All we can do is make a few small corrections, put the records into context for the user, and leave much of it in the imposed order[14] constructed by later custodians. This once natural informational ecosystem remains a rich ecosystem, just one a bit impoverished by the human hand.

I continuously fight against these artificial informational environments—or, at least, try to correct them via the practice of archival contextualization—yet I think must understand the value of archival zoos, just as we have traditionally accepted the value of animal zoos.[15] First, some records have been naturally segregated from their native ecosystem. They are already isolated, so assembling them in a series with other like pieces gives them a structure and a context. In other cases, there do exist quasi-natural collections, such as accumulations of autographs amassed by a single individual finding or writing to people whose signatures they desire. These may seem pointless to the archivist, who cannot understand how such an assemblage has any endearing value.[16] A person interested in humans bearing fame desires physical evidence of their true selves by amassing their signatures—yet why does this hobby matter? The answer is that human activity is both ordered and disordered, both deep and shallow, but also understandable and inscrutable—and the goal of archivists (as a whole, not in the case of any individual archivist) is to document the full range of human activity.

The world is messy and fallen, and it is not the archivist's job to return us to Eden. We don't even know what our Edens of records were. We must do our work with archives using the lightest touch necessary. Otherwise, we will artificialize collections ourselves, continuing the faulty practices of our predecessors.

I'm not making the case here for artificial collections—just for preserving the natural act of assembling information for a purpose, after that malady has already afflicted a set of records. In a manuscripts context, especially a century ago, many repositories collected or received individual documents, and there was an understandable reason for this. In the era, of the great man concept of history, the focus of attention and collection might naturally fall upon the individual "great" document, rather than on bulky

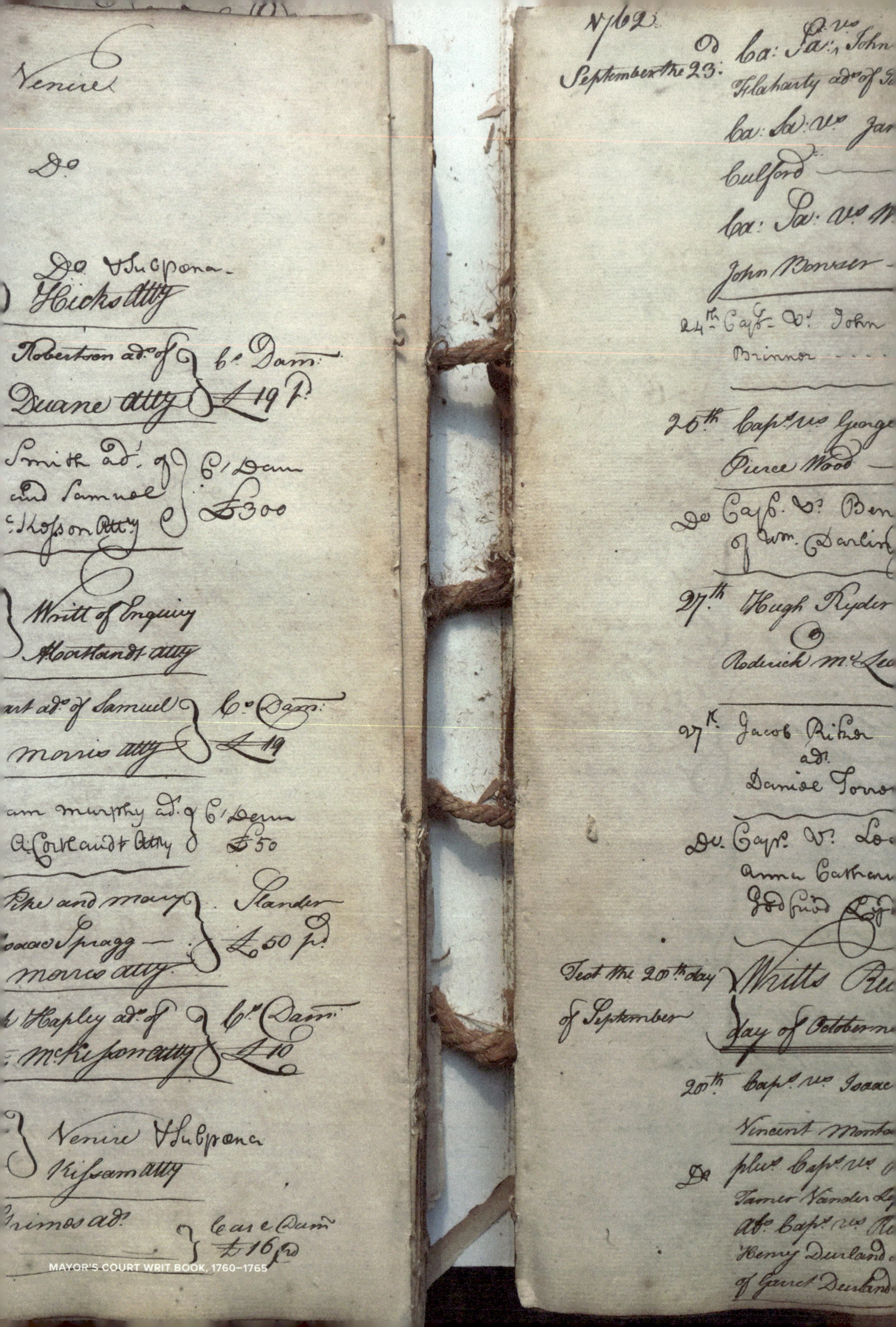

MAYOR'S COURT WRIT BOOK, 1760–1765

clusters of records that would overburden an ill-equipped manuscripts library. After such documents had accumulated in the library, the curator thought it better to create bodies of records—to form an informational ecosystem, no matter how shallow; to create a contextual construct to hold the records together. Just like a zoo, this environment is faux and lacking in genetic depth—but it also demonstrates a context of construction.

It has a creator, it has a purpose, it telegraphs a message of intention. It is not real, but neither is it quite counterfeit. It consists of a number of decontextualized artifacts the curator-creator has recontextualized. It carries the significance of intentional creation—if only after the fact of original creation. And, sometimes, we have to accept these bruised and bloodied quasi-fonds and recognize they now bear the marks of their middle past—the past lying between their beginning and the end of their change. We may have to respect that a past custodian has become a secondary creator. When we do, we will usually determine it is best to retain that new creation as it is and then demonstrate to users how such a chimerical creature came to live among our archives.

I do not celebrate these Frankenstinian pseudo-fonds, but we must live with them now, so we must accept, understand, and describe the degree to which these exhibit signs of natural development and to which they do not.

Archives deal with disappearances; they attempt to exorcise our fear of loss by amassing memory.

Wolfgang Ernst, *Stirrings in the Archives: Order from Disorder*, translated by Adam Siegel (Rowman & Littlefield: Lanham, 2015): 5.

#archivesquotes #context

An Archivist's Tail: Archives as Symbol

We are bound to and inspired by symbol. The real world continues to exist in its multifarious diversity. The solid earth rests beneath our feet. We breathe the air, we eat the earth's wheat, we pour huge cold drafts of water into our parched mouths—but it is symbol that moves us most, because our cultural representations of mere things and the hopes and aspirations and meanings we attach to these give them their power. The objects and concrete realities of our earth may be beautiful, even inspiring, in their own right, but it is the shared (and sometimes contrived) significance we apply to them that gives them their meaning, their power. Their glowing immanence comes from the light we have lit within them.

Even if we are not religious, we are forced to face the miracle of existence, the disturbing and comforting fact that we exist and a world of cornucopian richness surrounds us. We do not always recognize that we live within the ineffable. Being inhabitants of this space we realize that the earth and our place within it are not mundane, even if that observation sometimes slips out of our consciousness. Yet the fact of our unbelievable but evident existence allows us to accept that the ordinary is extraordinary, that mere things we can feel with our fingers may have a magic far beyond even the molecules that give them shape.

So it is with some records, though not with all of them. A record may be nothing but paper and ink,[1] but it can still carry emotional weight; it can still be both object and symbol, both the thing itself and the meaning within it that exceeds the meaning of its words. For a personal example, I once saw one half of the manuscript of James Joyce's novel *Finnegans Wake*, written in a language approximating English but filled with neologisms and other word formations that bore new meanings into the body of English. *Wake* is maybe the most difficult novel in English to read—deep knowledge of multiple European languages is necessary to give one enough purchase to figure out where this dream novel is moving—but because this novel plays so deeply with the workings of language, it is a touchstone for me. So I touched it. With ungloved fingers, for less than a second, merely to own the right to say I had.

To be sure, the obvious value of the manuscript was as a record of how Joyce wrote and edited this complicated novel, how he scratched out words and phrases, what he replaced them with, even how he physically wrote (large and rough). The manuscript allows us a certain narrow window into how he thought, how he created. But Joyce was the giant of 20th-century English language literature, a man whose work was both prized and despised, a weird human beast filled with gift and flaw. So to be in the presence of and to touch something he wrote (not the printed book but the scrawled original text), and something so significant, brings with it a sense of awe. Even though I knew the manuscript was just paper, ink, and pencil; just a human artifact—only a record of what had already passed. The record is not the event; it is the artifact created by a human event.

I have come to these thoughts of the importance of archives as symbol—and thus to the importance of symbolic value in archives over the course of a few months and a number of accidents of my presence.

The first of these was a talk by Brenda Cowan, of the Fashion Institute of Technology, on something she calls psychotherapeutic object dynamics. She explains her theory, in part, in this manner:

Grounding her study in the body of scholarship defining the phenomenological and evocative nature of objects, their influence in the lives of people, and the

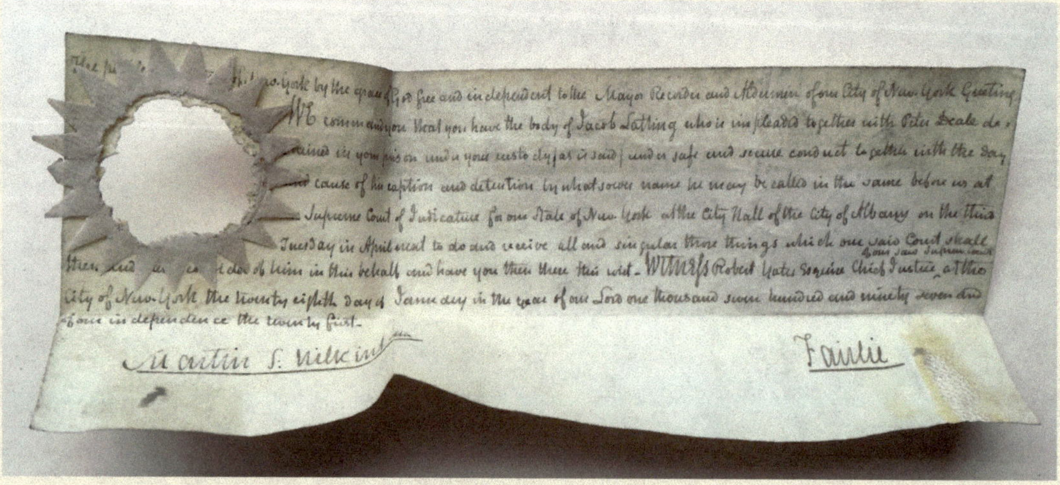
[illegible] of New York by the grace of God free and independent to the Mayor Recorder and Aldermen of our City of New York Greeting
WE command you that you have the body of Jacob Latting who is impleaded together with Peter Beale de-
tained in your prison under your custody (as it is said) under safe and secure conduct together with the day
and cause of his caption and detention by whatsoever name he may be called in the same before us at
Supreme Court of Judicature for our State of New York at the City Hall of the City of Albany on the third
Tuesday in April next to do and receive all and singular those things which our said Court shall
then and there [illegible] of him in this behalf and have you then there this writ — Witness Robert Yates Esquire Chief Justice of our said Supreme Court at the
City of New York the twenty eighth day of January in the year of our Lord one thousand seven hundred and ninety seven and
of our independence the twenty first —

SUPREME COURT OF JUDICATURE WRIT OF HABEAS CORPUS (1797)

characteristics that shape those meanings, she explored the reason for those meanings: their fundamental psychological underpinnings. Converging the disciplines of museum and object studies, psychology and psychotherapy, she followed the premise that people have an innate and necessary relationship with objects that she calls "primal dialogue," that is essential to personal meaning making and to an individual's psychological health.

Her field is museum studies, particularly exhibition design, so that is the starting point of her thinking. Museums are much more about objects than archives are, but almost all archives hold physical records, many hold non-record objects, and those that hold neither still keep digital objects. Although we conceptualize records as something different from artifacts, they are in fact artifacts, so much so that one archivist, long ago, suggested the term manufact to embrace the objectness of documents—and the recordness of objects.[2] Although Cowan is unlikely to have made a distinction between artifact and archive—because she would see a document as merely a type of artifact—her theory of the emotional resonance and therapeutic value of some artifacts can inform our thinking of the symbolic value of archives.

With my connection to Brenda, I sent her my essay on the symbolic significance of my most precious object, the only one I may never give up.[3] Her theory came into my mind a few months later at the annual symposium of the Archivists Round Table of Metropolitan New York, in a talk given by Marisa Hollywood of Queensborough Community College: "A Safe Space for Uncomfortable Conversations: The Kupferberg Holocaust Center and the Jacket from Dachau." Once again, the object in question was not documental. It was a jacket worn by a man held in a concentration camp during the Second World War, and what was amazing here was how the jacket was transformed into an object signifying survival rather than misery. I made a comment about psychotherapeutic object dynamics afterwards to the audience, and how archivists themselves need to consider this value of records.

Still, the references to symbolic value, which never included mention of the term, continued. When my wife, Karen Jamison Trivette, and I attended the International Council of Archives' SUV conference in Salamanca, Spain, I was entranced by Susanne Belovari's talk, "The ludicrous elephant's tail," which recounted the tale of the tail of Jumbo, likely the most famous elephant of all times. The Tufts University archives held this tail as a part of its archives, but it is ludicrous in many ways: the tail was not an elephant's tail but an obvious fake, it wasn't even the first of these fake tails, and it's not even a record, as used in our common sense. The stuffed remains of Jumbo were held by Tufts until they burned in a fire, but the fake tail represents that whole, and the important fact is this: the sports mascot of Tufts is Jumbo, so the tail itself—fake as it is—is a talisman, and

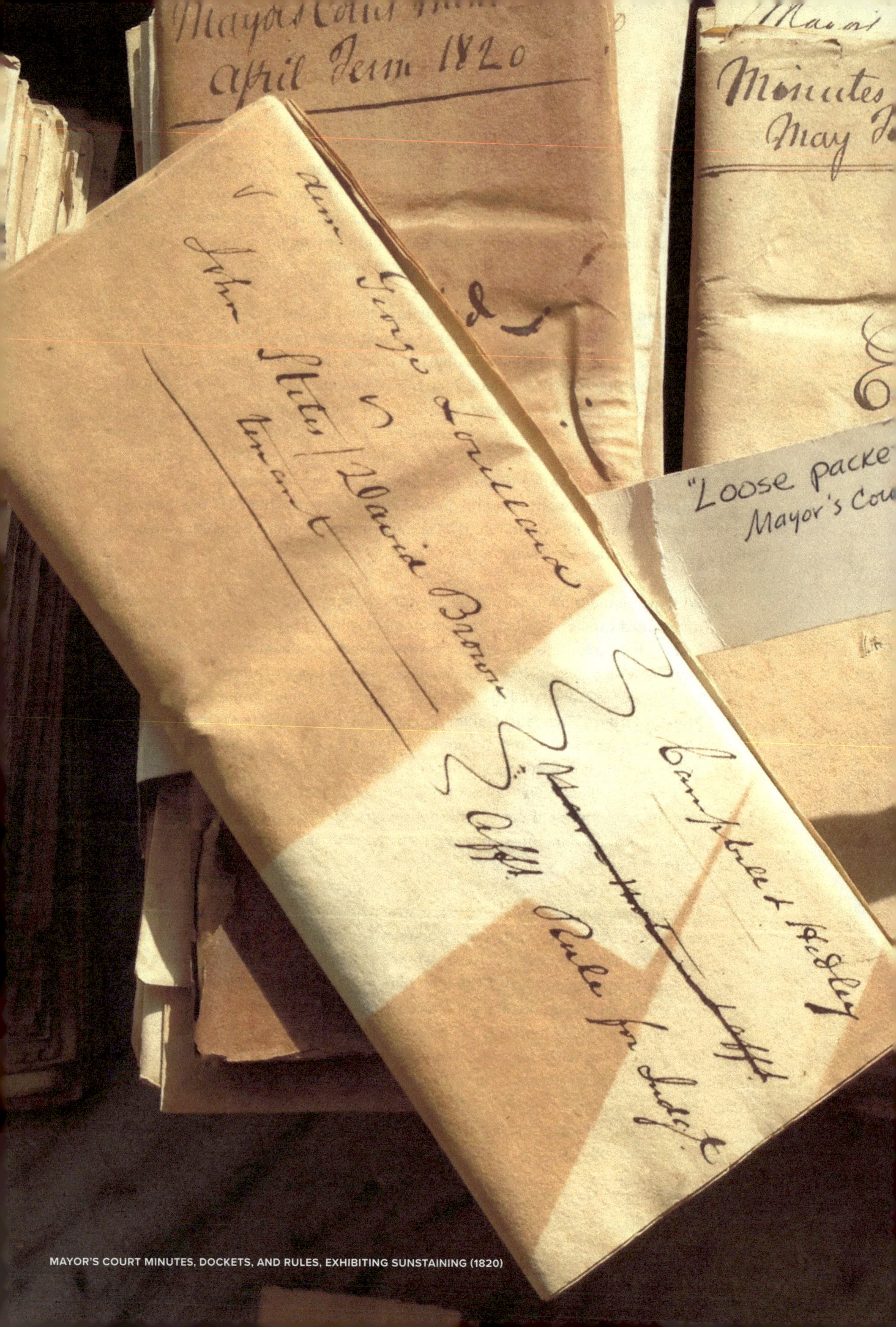

MAYOR'S COURT MINUTES, DOCKETS, AND RULES, EXHIBITING SUNSTAINING (1820)

a means by which the student body identifies itself and the reason by which they donate to the school as alumni.

Time and again, this issue arose. I attended the fall meeting of the Mid-Atlantic Regional Archives Conference this year and sat in a session on records of collegial sports—specifically because I have no interest in sports but I have interest in my friend Alan Delozier, who was speaking. What I learned was the value of sports memorabilia, whether record or artifact, and how that interest can actually help financially support an archives. A few weeks later, Kerri Anne Burke, Alan's wife, mentioned during the recording of a podcast of Karen's and mine that showing employees of Citi certain foundational or interesting documents literally connected them with their organization, even one that large.[4]

I don't overly care that the symbolic value of archives can help archives fund and support their operations, but we live in a world where money indicates value, so we should allow people to understand what they will value in the records of our organizations. We need to live in the real world, where money counts, but also where the heart guides where the money goes. We also need to guide ourselves by the heart as well as the head. Because the heart will tell the head where to go, and the heart will often be right. The only significant writing I've encountered discussing symbolic value was written by James O'Toole and published in 1993,[5] and O'Toole focused primarily on foundational documents, instead of the vast array of items, even non-records, held by archives.

Our interest in symbolic value must exceed the bounds of the Declaration of Independence and the Domesday Book. We must identify the symbolic value we personally feel and that we know others will feel. We must think broadly about the symbolic value different groups of users will find in our records. We must accept that the value of our records does not reside merely within the essential data they hold.

Value persists because of the visual traits, the historical resonance, and even the scent of records—diversifying its value beyond information alone. This value may require us to save records in their original forms because only the object carries this magic within it. We have to do this not just because we hope it will provide archives with money or interest others in our records. We must do this because we do our job well when we make it possible to realize all of the value and all the values of our records.

Digital documents last forever—or five years, whichever comes first.

Jeff Rothenberg, "Digital Information Lasts Forever—Or Five Years, Whichever Comes First," RAND Video V-079 (1997).

#archivesquotes #preservation #digitalrecords

Lacunae, Invisibility, and Other Archival Silences

It is the silence of the past that hurts me the most—its vacancy, its absence, the palpable loss. All the documented horrors of our previous presents may prove the venality of humanity, but I would rather know more of human depravity for a chance to know more of our past cultures, words, and thoughts.

In the notes for a presentation I am about to give about depersoning in colonial Manhattan, I write, "Because these records focused on men of privilege / They sometimes take the form of a congregation of silences." I doubt we often enough consider this kind of lacuna, one that is purposefully made without purposeful intent. The culture of early New York told men they were supreme, so these men made a society that certified them as such. (Of course, by *men* I mean white men, and particularly those of privilege, those owning property and of adequate wealth.) Given where they lived, in that milieu, they naturally, unconsciously, made records that provided little evidence of the presence of women.

Certainly, a woman could be found within the records of this colony (and in its later form as part of a republic), but usually only for crimes: selling alcohol to a slave, infanticide (quite rare), and, later, vagrancy—defined as having no honorable employment. But they do not often appear in the records for such acts, since men have always been more inclined to crime than women.

On the civil side of the judicial ledger, women did not often appear as parties in cases because they had very few civil rights—the primary one, in the English courts, was the right of dower, the right of a widow to one third of a deceased husband's estate. Women are most likely to be found in early civil records in divorce proceedings, but those were rare until the 1900s. Women could not be judges, sheriffs, or even jurors, so one can read hundreds of pages of a court minute book without running across a female name.

It is almost as if women did not exist in that society.

These injustices replicate themselves across the non-white spectrum of peoples as well, though black men make a reasonable number of appearances in some court records, which we know because the records themselves or their indexes often specifically define each of them by race. The null value, whiteness, goes unremarked, which allows society to classify all non-whites as the other, while protecting the primacy, the full rights of humanhood, to male whites.

Yet I do not mean these direct injustices to be the focus of my thinking about archival absence. They merely show one reason why absence prevails. By centering the recorded proceedings of society on one class of people (white men of privilege), we lose the story of that society as a whole. We can piece together what the culture was like—say, in the early 1700s when about 20 percent of the populace was slaves, mostly black but some of them Indian. We hear the stories of these people only in times of great crisis. We do not know in detail the breadth of experience of all the people who were living on a small strip of land at the bottom of this large island so long ago.

When we try to understand that past, we must fill in gaps, make assumptions, and sometimes create realities out of full cloth and thin air. We cannot simply

NEW YORK SUPREME COURT OF JUDICATURE WRIT, 1806. THIS WRIT IS ONE OF MANY IN THE ARCHIVES EATEN BY RODENTS, WHICH USUALLY ONLY ATE THE FLOUR PASTE THAT HELD PAPER SEALS TO PARCHMENT WRITS, BUT OCCASIONALLY THEY ATE THE PARCHMENT, ITSELF ORIGINALLY THE SKIN OF AN ANIMAL.

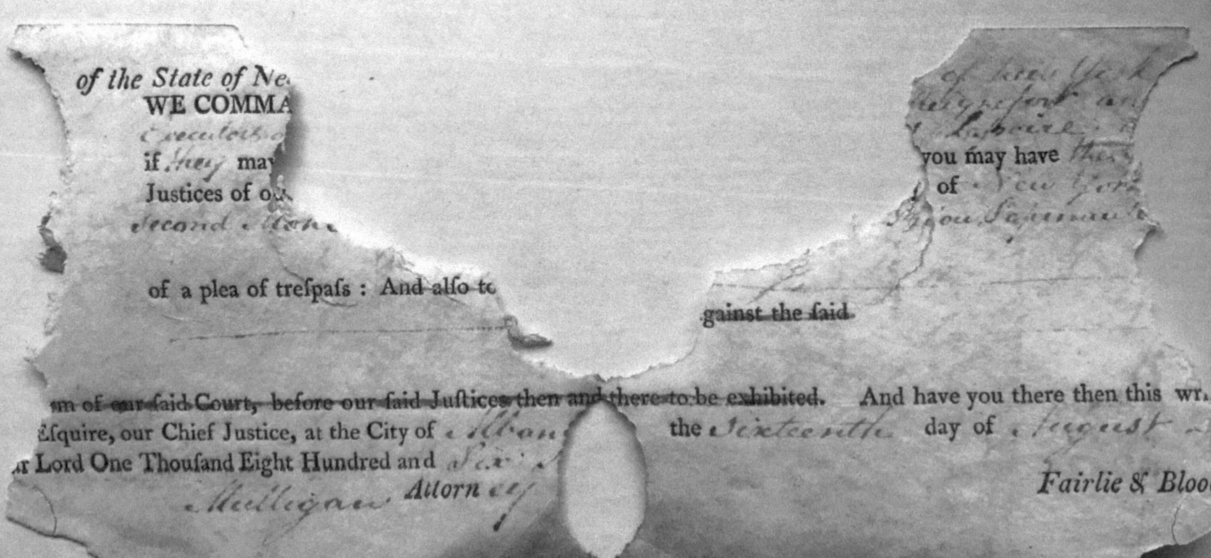

know. And archives are about allowing us to know, rather than guess; to see, instead of imagine. The silences deafen because we can hear nothing of them.

If no record is made, we have nothing to keep, nothing to refer to long after the fact. But sometimes records are made yet not kept. There is no simple system to identify every record a society must save to document itself and to ensure those records are maintained for use. You might say the word *appraisal*, even aloud, but that is just a process, not an inevitable system, such as the daily rising of the sun (during which the sun never moves).

We lose records because people do not want to save them, because they don't protect them, and because they cannot see the value they can bear into the future. Sometimes, people destroy records to extinguish the memories trapped within them. Other times, people store them in damp basements, allow them to be deleted from the cloud, or, in one case I knew well, stored them in a locked car in the heat and humidity of Florida.[1] Sometimes, storage conditions themselves destroy records or cause them to degrade. Both intent and accident bring an end to records.

Of course, some records must die. We simply want to save those few records that should live. We need an adequate sample of them.

A record is a fight against invisibility, or evidence of that struggle. It exists and by its existence it recounts a tale, provides information, allows for the possibility of insight. The record is made because someone wants it to be, but the length of its existence may be short or evidence of it hidden. In an era of data and flux, one where we can find the digital footprints of almost anyone we know without leaving our desks, people yearn for invisibility, privacy, the silencing of their presences. Our future will continuously be more and more about balancing access and privacy, existence and absence. The world where saving is naturally good and valuable is passing. We moving to a time where every decision must be made upon a scale.

I still want more records to survive. As evidence, I have saved even embarrassing records about myself because I didn't want to disturb too greatly the story of my life. You can find them in my personal papers.[2] Nothing is hidden from view. All is open. No restrictions. But that is merely a personal preference of someone often very open, but still someone considerably hidden. Openness is not itself a sure sign of openness.

We live in a world of degrees, not absolutes.

We also live in a world with a fractured and fragmented past, one that we cannot quite see back into. In my own work as an archivist, I frequently encounter records that have broken physically apart: records ripped in half, shot through with a pellet gun, blackened by oil, eaten by rodents, and records so brittle they had cracked into pieces. Sometimes, I can find the fragments and return them to a simulacrum of wholeness, yet often their fragmentation endures, irreversibly.

In the case of one 1806 writ I found, a rodent had chewed all four edges of the folded writ, so that when opened it appeared to be a physical Rorschach test, where the mirroring remainder of the writ was the ink we needed to decipher and the actual text fell out away from our senses as insignificant noise. So much of the text was gone, the actual words held but limited meaning. I could identify the court only by the names of its clerks ("Fairlie & Blood[good]"), yet I retained this document.

There may be a time in the future when this sturdy fragment—because parchment is sturdy—will answer a question.

But maybe not.

We hold onto these fragments not because of the information they provide but because of what they hold back. We retain them because they are a physical message from the past, even when that message is one we do not want to hear:

We are no longer here.

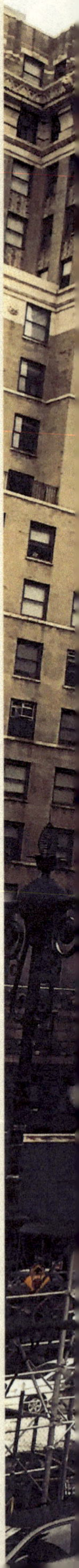

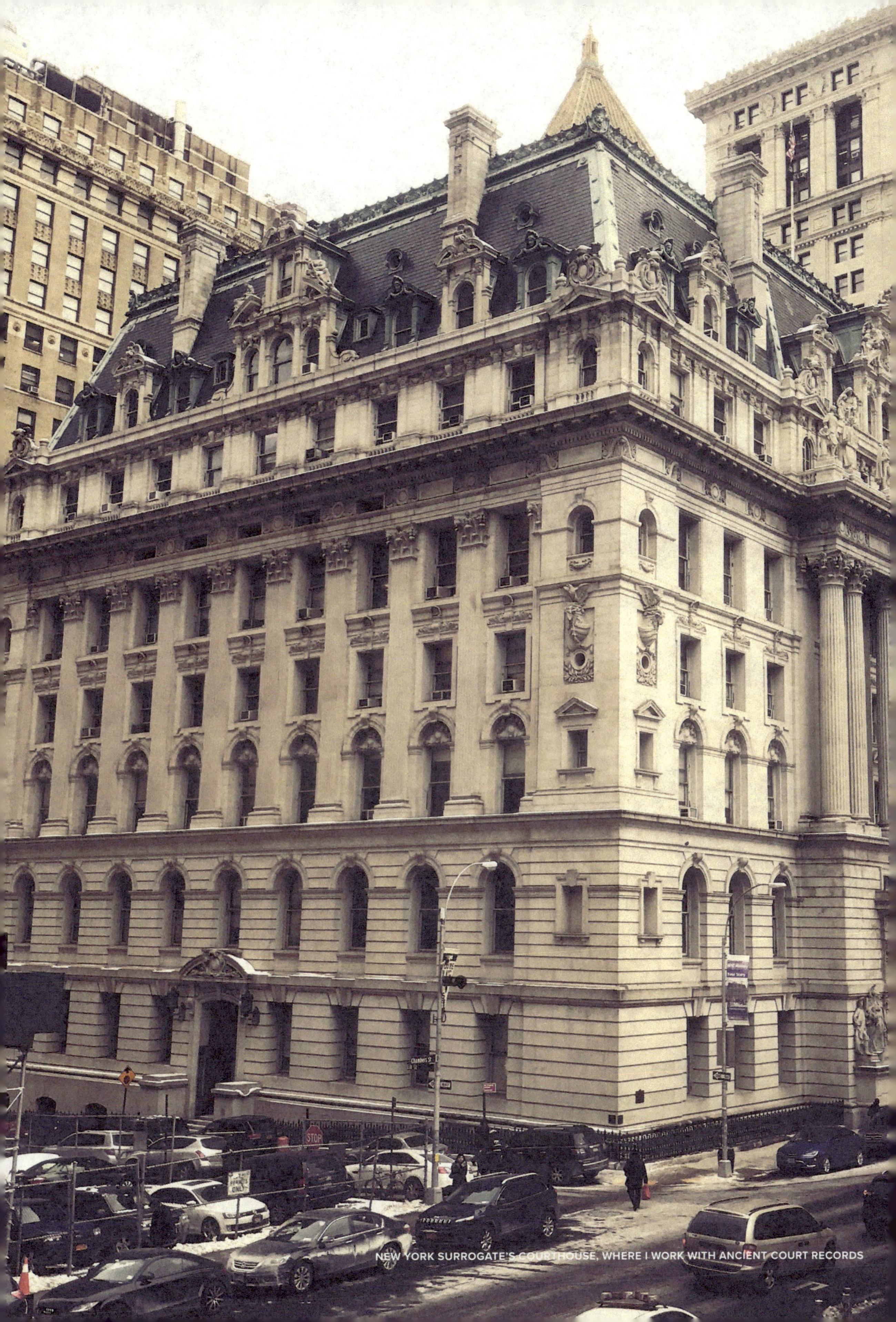

NEW YORK SURROGATE'S COURTHOUSE, WHERE I WORK WITH ANCIENT COURT RECORDS

The activism surrounding tribal archives is a direct response to the historical effects that exclusion, annihilation, and discrimination have had on Native Americans communities, traditional lifeways, and culture since the European colonization of North America.

Jennifer R. O'Neal, "'The Right to Know': Decolonizing Native American Archives," *Journal of Western Archives* 6:1:2. (2015): 4.

#archivesquotes #decolonization

The Slave Revolt of 1712: The Provision and Omission of Justice in Early New York

This is a story about a failed struggle for freedom,[1] but it is also a story about archives—one about their value and about their limitations to show us the past.

My attempt here is, first, to show the culture of these early inhabitants of Manhattan—rather than merely tell the stories that illustrate that culture. Second, I'm trying to understand this story without resorting to sources outside these records. Mine is a thought experiment, one that interrogates the value of archives as the historical record. I'm trying to determine what these archives actually do for us. As an archivist, I'll be telling this story through the court records of early New York, trying to discover what the record unintentionally tells us, and assessing the authenticity and reliability of that record.

The event I am examining we generally call a revolt, but I give it another name, because this revolt was truly a short-lived and failed revolution. It was an unsuccessful battle for freedom by an enslaved people or, maybe, peoples—for the people fighting and dying for freedom were black, indigenous, mixed race, men, and women.

As an archivist, I know the record is not simply an encrustation of truth. I also realize truth can come to us through the record. My goal here is to find whatever truth I can.

The minute book of the Court of General and Quarter Sessions of the Peace (1694–1731), a defunct county-level criminal court,[2] is the only source I used to create this account. The volume is wrapped in vellum and written in the hand of its age. This alone helps us accept this book as authentic, as truly what it says it is, and other evidence supports that conclusion, including its provenance. These records came from the court itself. They were transferred to the custody of the New York County Commissioner of Records probably near 1855, and in 1942 they were transferred to the custody of the New York County Clerk.

But how reliable is this record? How believable are the facts presented within its pages? For the most part, quite so—as a record of how people were judged and what decisions the jury made. But we know little about how and why the jury made those verdicts, and we don't know exactly what information they left out or why, but we can see the shapes of absences within its pages: We do not usually know when the convicted were executed. We do not learn many of the details of the killings that initiated the trials. We cannot determine, in the end, if the verdicts were fair, even by the standards of that time.

I discovered evidence of the slave revolt accidentally in the index at the front of these minutes. This phrase jumped out at me:

Negro slaves for ye: Murder of

Seven times repeated, it was a magical number and a portentous phrase, and I heard it as a chant running in my head. These cases of murder were sandwiched between a case of assault and one for keeping a disorderly house (a house of prostitution). That there were many slaves in New York at the time was no surprise. New York was a big slave state, for a northern one. Blacks and slaves do not often appear in these minute books, and when they do, they are usually nameless, usually bit actors, but always central to the story. The minutes refer to them when others are accused of crimes, such as entertaining slaves, allowing them to drink alcohol in their "tippling houses," or selling something to them. Slaves were those people from whom this society kept not just freedoms, but also any pleasures.[3] Note that these slaves were not contained in one spot, as slaves were on southern plantations. The slaves of early New York often had to move about in the city to complete their tasks, and that is how they became entangled in crimes of pleasure.

Murders were rare in this society, and indictments of slaves were rarer still—so this is not a usual story from this version of Manhattan.

The entries in this book documenting this revolution begin on page 212 and end on page 248, taking up only 37 pages. Within those few pages is the story of the punishments meted out for the insurrection, but the book doesn't treat this event as a revolt at all. It simply presents charges of murder and records punishments and acquittals. The book reflects its makers, so it merely demonstrates the operation of the state against individuals, not the action of one people against another people. White New Yorkers running the trials must have seen this battle for what it was—an attempt at revolution, and one that frightened them, that caused even them to worry for their lives.

To understand what transpired during the revolution and the following trials, we must interpret the formulaic text of the book's entries, while knowing few details of the killings or the human struggle for freedom that led to those. This struggle or uprising is kept secret by the court clerks who wrote in this volume, yet it is obvious to us now. We can read even what is not written in the volume.

What you need to know about this minute book is that it is engrossed. In short, this means it was written after the fact, after the trials concluded. The original practice of this court (and of other courts of this era) was to write hurried and rudimentary minutes during its proceedings and to transcribe those later—when they would complete the record by adding the required juridical language and detail and by writing the entries out in clean, clear, crisp script. (The rough minutes for these years, by the way, no longer exist, so we do not know what information the original scrawled notes contained.) These engrossed minutes are written in full, but entries don't always appear in chronological order, leading to possible questions of their reliability. Yet is it truly important that a rewriting of a text be written into a book in chronological order? To assume it is, are we merely substituting our contemporary inclinations for those of centuries ago? It is hard to be sure, but maybe the order of entries also helped indicate the relative importance to this society of each case heard.

A set of "memoranda" for the trials cluster after the entries outlining the trials themselves. I have not found other instances of memoranda elsewhere in the minutes of this or any other court, which may indicate these trials were so unusual the courts created or revived practices specifically to address these cases. The memoranda detail each individual case from indictment to sentencing, so they provide the entire story arc of a case in one densely written spot. Only these memoranda give us any details of the killings people are accused of, such as weapons employed in the killings. We don't see this information elsewhere in the minutes or in any other records.

One of these memoranda recounts the first case in the series of related trials held before the court, that of Clause, Robin, Quaco, and Sam. This trial began on the 11th of April 1712, merely four days after the revolt itself, which we know because the memorandum tells us the "murder" occurred on that day "in the Eleventh year of the Reign of our Soveraign [*sic*] Lady Anne." What we also know—though we don't ever quite know why—is that this is the most important trial, apparently because it was the most egregious killing. We assume this because this case came first and because of the various and unusually barbaric methods the colony employed to execute most of these men:

Clause be broke alive upon a wheel and so to Continue languishing until he be dead and his head and Quarters to be at the Queens [*sic*] disposal

Robin be hung up in Chains alive and so to Continue without any sustenance until he be dead and Consumed

Quaco be burnt with fire until he be dead and Consumed

Sam be hanged by the neck until he be dead

The most serious crime was tried first. The most serious criminals were executed in the worst ways. The minutes tell us this without mentioning these facts.

The slaves were almost always executed off stage, their actual deaths unrecorded in the minutes. Only occasionally is an execution noted in the margins of the volume, but we are always told how the accused will die—because "Guilty" is merely the finding of the court. The manner of execution is the true sentence for those found guilty.

In most cases, death is by hanging. In select cases, a more serious punishment of slow burning is employed: "burned with a slow fire that he may Continue in Torment for Eight or ten hours & Continue burning. . .until he be dead and Consumed to Ashes." The details of the punishments mattered because they indicated the severity of the crime. The details feel like vengeance. Only in the case of Clause was anyone broken on a wheel, his head and quarters offered to the Queen. His was a painful and gruesome manner of death, suggesting he was the ringleader of the group, even though no evidence is given anywhere directly implicating Clause in a conspiracy. Robin, though, receives probably what is the worst death, and possibly because the jurors identified him as the killer, though the record never mentioned this: to hang by chains, exposed to the elements, likely with arms splayed, until he starved to death.

Which brings us to Justice. To the colony's credit, it did practice some form of justice. Not every slave indicted by the grand jury was found guilty; of those charged, just over a half were convicted. It is ironic, though, that a society grudgingly recognizing the humanity of those within it who were not white would accuse these slaves of acting "Traytereously." The slaves received no protection from the Crown. They had no country to betray, yet they still could somehow be tried as traitors. Of course, we could never have hoped for fairness when those being tried were already slaves.

Still, we can glimpse in these records the process of creating a system of justice. Grand juries convened to review evidence of crimes: the dates of actions and names of the accused, the type of weapon used (a gun or knife) and its monetary value (because everything in this capitalistic society was measured in cash), the length and breadth of the mortal wound (an example of the court's early forays into forensics), and the time it took death to arrive (always given as "immediately," though likely never so). The accused could also plead "Not Guilty" and give exculpatory statements, so the accused had a voice in their trials.

Justice was swift, if not quite true.

Because of the scarcity of evidence presented in the minutes, it is difficult to identify reasons for the court's decisions. So I organized the data into tables so I could better evaluate the data on these trials. Using these tools, I quickly determined that 21 of 39 people indicted were found guilty; all of those were black, two of them women; each of the three Indian slaves was acquitted, as was the one slave identified as mulatto; and half the women were exonerated.

Interest in the trials, or the strength of the cases themselves, petered out by the end, maybe because the last three people indicted carried greater status than the others. Since no owner was listed for any them, they must have been free, and they had surnames, or the approximation of such: John Harris, Peter the Porter, and Peter the Doctor. The first was acquitted and paid his own fees, and

SUPREME COURT OF JUDICATURE CIVIL AND CRIMINAL PARCHMENTS (1684–1848)

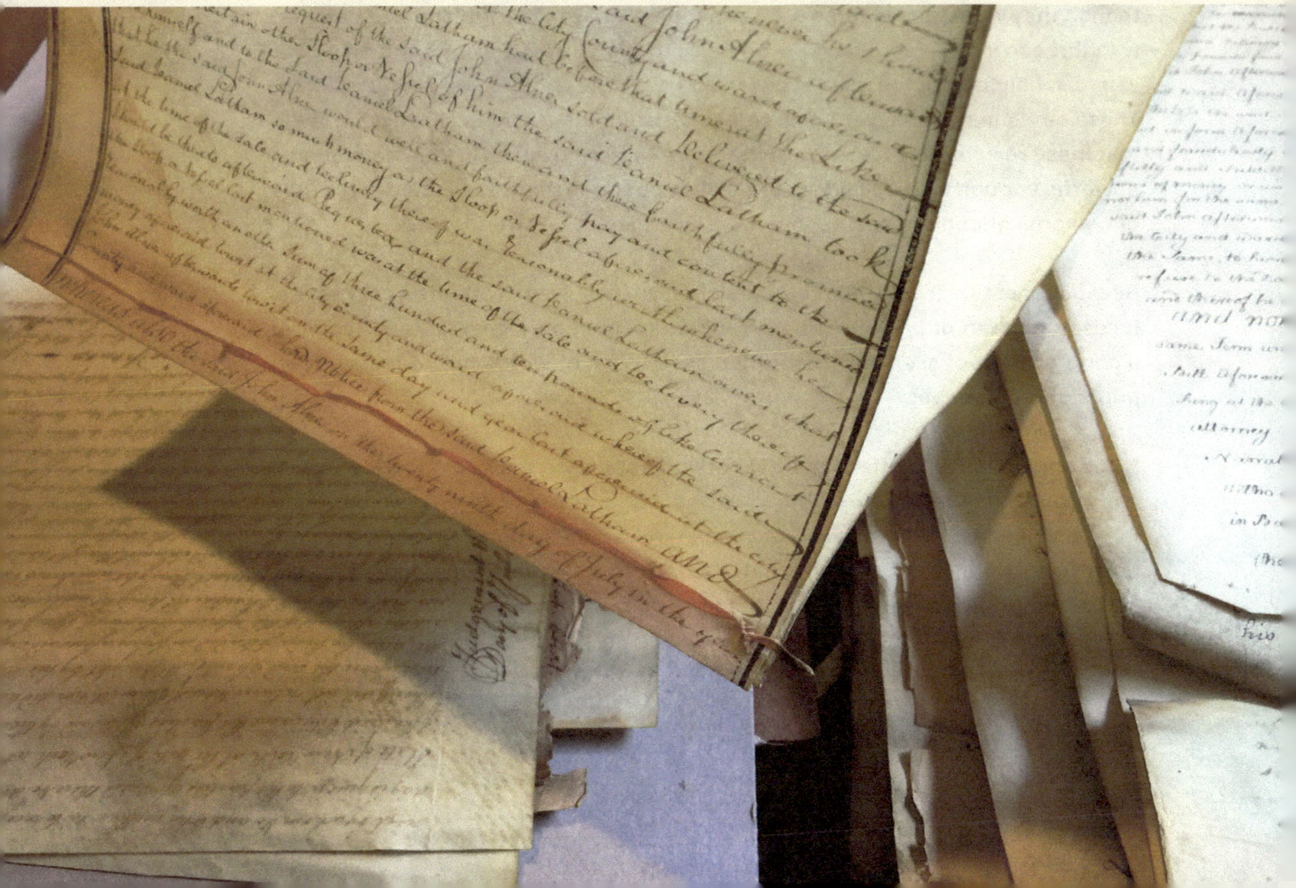

according to the records, the two Peters were simply "not tried." These results at the very end of the trials appear to support the idea that the most serious cases were tried first, and the least important were saved for the end—and essentially abandoned.

While reviewing these cases, I looked for possible biasing factors in the jury's decisions. I tried to determine if the juries treated female slaves more generously. They did not: about half of the men and exactly half of the women were convicted. I wondered if the slaves of widows received better treatment, and these slaves were acquitted at a slightly higher rate than others, suggesting these slaves may have been spared to allow them to continue to care for those widows. No Indian slave was found guilty, which may be a sign of leniency to this group or evidence that black male slaves led this revolt.

In most trials, some slaves were found guilty and others not, which suggests jurors did deliberate. They did not merely convict everyone charged. What we don't know is whether the verdicts were truly determined by an examination of the facts as presented or if the most important factor in play was the identity and status of the slave owner—either the one killed or the one whose slaves were on trial. We cannot merely assume justice when we learn that in two trials all the defendants were found guilty when in another trial every slave accused of Joris Maerschalek's killing was either found not guilty or not even tried.

Most interestingly, none of Jacob Regnier's five slaves was found guilty, even though they were tried in three separate trials and even though one was charged with three murders, more than anyone else accused. This was also the only case where multiple indicted slaves owned by a single person were all acquitted. These cases may be signs of bias or innocence or luck. It seems likely, however, that these results indicate some of these men were powerful in their community, powerful enough to keep and secure their property in the face of murder charges or powerful enough to ensure they were avenged even after death.

Because most of the extant court records of early New York are civil records focused on men of privilege, these records courts sometimes take the form of a congregation of silences, rather than sequences of words or the telltale footprints of ink on paper.

Black and Indian inhabitants of New York do appear on the pages of New York's early court records but only when charged with a crime or when others treated them as humans. The regulation of order required these people be depersoned, uncitizened, invisible, but it was not just race that divided people into categories of power. Even a simple panel of jurors demonstrates men had agency, that men of acceptable race and stature could sit in judgment of others. For that reason, the records record these white men, and we know who they were, where they lived, what they did as a trade. We know little about the women, who rarely appear on these pages (and usually only for running a disorderly house). Women could not sit as jurors, and in this culture women lost the last name they had left (their first) when their husbands died and those names were replaced with "Widow."

In these criminal cases related to this uprising, we are told essentially nothing about the men and women charged with murder. They are as hidden and silent as widows, yet more so.

The volume holding the records of the slave trials is brittle and fragmented. In some cases, words along the edges of the pages are missing, but the text is still clear. Its signal from the past remains steady, just a bit hazy, yet it is incomplete. It tells one slender thread of the story very well, but it hews to a narrow path, and its details are evasive. We must make sense of the text on our own, via the context of the era and the minutes themselves, by processing the data within, by holding the text up to the light to see through it into the past. We must take this disarrayed past and give it structure. We have to divine the connections between events. In the end, these minutes do not quite recount the history of this time or even of these trials; they merely reveal something of their aura.

The novelist William Faulkner famously wrote, "The past is never dead. It's not even past." But much of the past is past, irrevocably so. Records can tell us only so much before going silent.

The only pasts that remain are the remembered and the recorded pasts—and a less often considered past: the echoed past, one we live every day but don't necessarily see the outlines of, one built up by the history that preceded us, one invisible but still palpable. This past is the continuation of a culture, how a society may change yet still drag all the ills of its ancient preoccupations and preconceptions into the present.

That is the past we live every day. It is muffled a bit by time and erosion, but we all still live huddled at the very bottom of Manhattan—our viewshed: the ocean that stretches back to Europe. And we just might never leave.

Archives and their use enable a cycle of storytelling with multiple characters and perspectives, different endings, and even never-endings.

Tanya Zanish-Belcher, "Keeping Evidence and Memory: Archives Storytelling in the Twenty-First Century," *The American Archivist* 82:1 (Spring/Summer 2019): 10.

#archivesquotes #stories

endnotes

MINIATURES (DONE WHILE IN HIDING)

1. Tom Fuchs, personal conversation, (Ta-Boo, Palm Beach, Florida, 17 February 2020); Fuchs, Valerie, SPARC Connect, Fashion Institute of Technology, https://atom-sparc.fitnyc.edu/fuchs-valerie (visited 21 March 2020).

2. But it's not clear if she hid with her husband, her sister, or alone—three stories exist in her papers and its description, and I have not determined via the records alone which is the true story, or if all of them were true, only at different times. I haven't tried to clarify, because this story does not require that detail to meet its own needs for accuracy.

3. Fuchs, Valerie, SPARC Connect, Fashion Institute of Technology, https://atom-sparc.fitnyc.edu/fuchs-valerie (visited 21 March 2020).

4. Tom called these "doodles," as does the finding aid, but the binder that holds these drawings identifies these as "Miniatures (done while in hiding)," which sequence of words I have repurposed as the title of this essay.

5. This was not her only means of forgetting the world around her. She also said, "I found a lot of old and broken toys stored in there. So I mended them to pass the times. I'd taken art at school, and my father had sent me to Vienna to study fashion designing, so I was good at using my hands." Florence De Santis, "Glove Designer Led Cloak and Dagger Existence," [Albany] *Times-Union*, undated newspaper clipping, Valerie Fuchs collection, circa 1940–1986.

6. According to a newspaper article, all Fuchs' "personal belongings were in a bag which she would take into the hole with her at a moment's notice." Florence De Santis, "Glove Designer Led Cloak and Dagger Existence," [Albany] *Times-Union*, undated newspaper clipping, Valerie Fuchs collection, circa 1940–1986.

7. "Fuchs took even the postwar Communist coup in her stride. She used her knowledge of hiding out to get herself across the border, joined her husband in England, and finally arrived in the United States." Florence De Santis, "Glove Designer Led Cloak and Dagger Existence," [Albany] *Times-Union*, undated newspaper clipping, Valerie Fuchs collection, circa 1940–1986.

8. Tom Fuchs, personal conversation, (Ta-Boo, Palm Beach, Florida, 17 February 2020).

9. As of 24 March 2020, according to the New York *Times*, this number is 14,904, and the total number of infections has been doubling every three days. ("New York's case count is doubling every three days, the governor says," New York *Times*, 24 March 2020, https://www.nytimes.com/2020/03/24/world/coronavirus-news-live-updates.html).

DISCOVERING & JOY OF BECOMING

1. Let me note here that I have not conducted the research to make this statement, hence the weaseliness of my phrasing. I create entries and write definitions for the *Society of American Archivists' Dictionary of Archives Terminology*, and because of this I have a relatively deep understanding of archival terminology and how it has developed and changed over the years. But I've never studied the word "discovery" to see when we began to use this term (and its children: discovery tool, discovery process, etc.). Often, people make broad statements about language they cannot support with facts, and this may indeed be one. I will admit, for instance, that I've just found a 1961 use of discovery that seems to fit this archival sense—but I'm not sure, yet, that it carries that facet of meaning it has in our contemporary context.

2. The discovery of these writs wasn't a significant one (I'd seen thousands of such writs by then), but I loved finding five years' worth of writs created on behalf of the lawyer Quackenbush in one place and revealing the original—and otherwise almost totally unknown—arrangement used by the court clerks who first managed these records. Finding these gave me insight into the workings of the Supreme Court of Judicature and had the value of radiating the aura of beauty that disintegration can sometimes have.

3. Alas, I have never written down my entire conceptual grounding for archives, so this will only be a peek into my thoughts on it. I think archivists have finally accepted that any intellectual pursuit—of which archives definitely is one—

requires conceptual theorization to inform actual practice. It is good for us as workers and good for the profession as well. Theory dispels the idea that we are pullers of records, rather than knowledge workers intent on increasing knowledge across the spectrum of human activity.

4. Unlike my friends in the world of information governance, I eliminate the step of "wisdom" from the information continuum (my term), which moves forward in complexity and value in this order: data, information, records, knowledge, wisdom. I am wary of the term wisdom and unsure any human truly achieves wisdom. We most likely achieve proficiency or excellence—but in narrow aspects of our lives, and likely for limited ranges of time. Also, the word wisdom always forces me to think of wizard, which makes the use of the former too goofy for my tastes. In case you were wondering, Yes, wisdom and wizard ramify from the same root.

5. Occasional readers of my small essays strewn over the internet, may perceive a correlation between the concept of potential and kinetic knowledge and a concept I have written about: the potential and kinetic value of records. This similarity is intentional, and it points to the deep purpose of archives—to make active (not activist, I'll note) change for the benefit of humanity; to ensure archivists are not waiting for patrons to appear at their door but actively encouraging them to enter; to ensure all archivists see their work is active intellectual work designed to help people know more, think more deeply, and help all of us understand and better the world. (This does not remove the obvious fact that people will use archives to make the world worse and to try to diminish the biological stores of information residing in our heads with non-facts, distortions, and lies—but we cannot allow the bad to murder the best.)

6. Let me say, in another of my lengthy asides, that this intellectual breakthrough may be a small one, a personal one that affects one person or only a few. But it is still a breakthrough and still the creation of knowledge. Despite my heady sermons on knowledge, I treasure small bits of knowledge as much as the life-changing ones. Because every discovery is a new discovery. I do not honor the work of historians writing books over those of genealogists tracking down ancestors or grassroots activists looking for information on environmental changes to their part of the country. To the archivist, any research—no matter how apparently unimportant to us personally—is work we should honor, because we do not know what value that knowledge will eventually have and because allowing users access to the records they want confirms their work and gives them the pleasure of being recognized as living, thinking creatures of our own kind. Okay, even this is a bit highfalutin—and that is because I believe in giving people the agency they need to make their lives what they want them to be.

7. I will note, however, that I am a strong proponent of active archivy, in which we ensure the records our institutions need are created. That is a story for another day, but archivists as active creators—in the form of oral history programs and active inciteful documentary programs, for example—are heroic figures in my mind. They identify gaps in the historical record and ensure the creation of records to fill those gaps. But most of us do not continuously assume the role of creator in our lives as archivists.

8. Take, for instance, the word "literally," which literally means "literally"—and its opposite, "figuratively." This drives purists mad, because they want every word to have one true meaning. Problem is monosemous words are rare, consisting only of those words very rarely used. For instance, the word "archives," by my count—and I've done extensive research on this—has at least 11 separate nounal senses in the archives world—and I could add to at least one other from outside of our universe. So how are we supposed to know what "literally" means? one might ask, and I have two answers to that, the first tautological (but how else are we going to learn?):

1. "Literally" literally means "literally."

Okay, not too helpful, so here is a second:

2. We are archivists, so the answer is staring us in the face. We know what it means by the context in which it occurs. If this is how records mean (via context), and records significantly consist of words, then why can't it work for words themselves?

9. Rick Rojas, "Centuries of New York History Prepare for a Move," New York *Times* (5 January 2017), https://www.nytimes.com/2017/01/05/nyregion/new-york-documents-archives-records.html. (Or see the paper version published on 6 January 2017 on page A15.) Note that the subheading to the article begins with "Caked with dust."

10. Geof Huth, "Let Me Tell You About Aaron Burr's Divorce: Promoting Archives through the Media," *Archival Outlook* (January/February 2019): 10, 23.

11. Which point of view I'm guessing (not asserting—because I don't really know) I share with only a small percentage of archivists.

12. I live in the real world, so I know people can be a pain in the neck, but they are sometimes the best thing that will ever happen to us.

DIRT

1. However, archival storage at the University at Albany and the New York State Archives are spotless—those storage areas were merely not the places where I worked.

2. This clause seems quite dated now, even though I still receive the occasional piece of personal correspondence in an envelope.

3. My job now encompasses many archives, most of which are reasonably clean. However, this one was created so early that people really did not know how to store records efficiently, which means managing order in that space would require us to rip out all the "state-of-the-art" storage cabinets set up in 1911—and still be left with a building inefficiently built for the storage of records.

4. The last episode of the podcast *Serial* spends about a minute discussing part of this space and referring to one section of it as the "Mad Hatter's archive room" (*Serial*, Episode 12, 18 December 2014, minute mark 25:15).

5. Although I never remember to use these.

REMEMBERING THE FUTURE: THE CORE RELEVANCE OF ARCHIVES

1. I began this essay in 2015 while reading *The American Archivist* 78:1 (Spring/Summer 2015). I recently found my notes for this penciled in the issue in Sharon A. Weiner, Sammie Morris, and Lawrence J. Mykytiuk's article, "Archival Literacy Competencies for Undergraduate History Majors" on page 156 (where I wrote the original title and first two sentences of the essay) and on the title page (where I rewrote the title, transforming the original title into the current subtitle). I did this while reading through the entire issue, front to back, as was my process then. Unbeknownst to me at the time, my opening two-sentence paragraph was merely a reworking of the motto of Jack Welch, one of the most famed CEOs of General Electric (which corporation was based in Schenectady when I moved there in 1988 but not when I exited in 2015): "Forget the Past, Love the Future" (as quoted in Paul C. Lasewicz's article, "Forget the Past? Or History Matters? Selected Academic Perspectives on the Strategic Value of Organizational Pasts"). My future-focusing in this essay, however, likely bears little resemblance Welch's, whose ideas encapsulated in that quotation merely roused my own meandering and sometimes subconscious thinking on this issue over my decades as an information professional interested in making the case for the value of archives to society and humanity as a whole.

2. Along with other duties: records manager, librarian, poet—they all fit together, but that's a story for another day.

3. A term so fraught in our profession it is often difficult to know what we mean by using it.

4. For this is the work I do myself.

5. Since the context of a record or series or fonds continues over time, records continue to accrue contextual underpinnings even long after the decease or termination of the creator. This type of context I call *extranatural*, since *supernatural* would give it unintended meanings. I considered the terms *native* and *extra-native*, but the latter struck me as unnatural English (as did the possible *extra-organic*.

STUFF AND NON-STUFF

1. "stuff, n.1," OED Online, December 2018, Oxford University Press, http://www.oed.com (accessed December 27, 2018).

2. This phrase itself ("archival materials") is a generic term we use—especially when referring to the entire universe of such materials.

3. Sure, sure, we call it the "archival bond," that connection between records that holds them intellectually and functionally together. I just wanted to phrase it differently here.

4. As of today (28 December 2018), I recognize a dozen separate senses of the word *archives*, some singular and some plural in nature: Three are senses of *archives* as records, two as selections or collections of records or surrogates of same, one as non-records managed as archives, four as facilities or organizations used to manage archives, and one as our profession itself. With any luck, I'll eventually pare this down to ten.

5. See "The Content of Context" in this volume.

6. Kathy Roe Coker, "Short Subjects: User Statistics and Records Appraisal," *Provenance, Journal of the Society of Georgia Archivists* 3:1 (1985): 104.

7. Leon J. Stout, "Reimagining Archives: Two Tales for the Information Age," *The American Archivist* 65:1 (Spring/Summer 2002): 21.

8. Aaron D. Purcell, *Donors and Archives: A Guidebook for Successful Programs* (Rowan & Littlefield: Lanham, Md., 2015): xix.

9. Dorothy Waugh, Review of *The Science of Managing Our Digital Stuff* by Ofer Berman and Steve Whittaker, *The American Archivist* 81:1 (Spring/Summer 2018): 233.

10. Richard J. Cox, "The Archivist and Collecting: A Review Essay," *The American Archivist* 59:4 (Fall 1996): 498.

11. Mark A. Greene, "What Were We Thinking? A Call to Embrace Reappraisal and Deaccessioning," *Provenance, Journal of the Society of Georgia Archivists* 20:1 (2002): 35.

12. Kate Theimer, "What is the Professional Archivist's Role in the Evolving Archival Space? (Society of Georgia Archivists Annual Meeting Keynote Address, 2014)," *Provenance, Journal of the Society of Georgia Archivists* 32:1 (2014): 23.

13. Can I actually say such things? Well, first, I'm my own editor here, so I can do what I want. Second, these are facts, and, third, I don't mean these as insults but as observations. And I'll note that I was as dismayed as any archivist upon hearing how Mark Greene, weakened by illness, died in a horrific car crash.

14. And one taken far too soon from us. I had seen Cook at the Society of American Archives many times, but I do

not believe I ever decided I had enough to talk to him about to bother him. Still, losing such a giant in the profession at such a relatively early age, and one who focused his career—as have I—on government records was another sharp los for me. Sometimes, the people we don't know are the hardest ones to give back to nothingness.

15. Terry Cook, "The 'English Report' and Archives: A Critical Appreciation," *Archivaria* 53 (Spring 2002): 120.[17] I'm not including in this discussion the thematic collections of books I have donated to the University at Albany, but rest assured there are thousands of them.

16. <Decode> Artists Policing Data, Anna and Andrew Shiva Gallery, John Jay College of Criminal Justice, New York, NY, 28 November 2018 – 18 January 2019.

17. To use a word the OED last found in this sense from 1624. "objectual, adj.," OED Online, December 2018, Oxford University Press, http://www.oed.com.dbgateway.nysed.gov/view/Entry/129650?redirectedFrom=objectual (accessed December 28, 2018).

WHEN DEPATRIATION IS REPATRIATION

1. Which makes up roughly one half of my life.

2. Which is nine years after the creation of the English courts of the British colony of New York.

3. In an unsettling coincidence, the longest serving county clerk of New York County (AKA Manhattan), Norman Goodman, died today. The New York *Times* wrote a detailed obituary of him, but one focused on his work as the commissioner of jurors and only tangentially addressing his responsibilities as the master overseer of the oldest English and American court records of Manhattan. (The New York State Archives and the New York City Municipal Archives respectively hold the oldest colonial and city court records from the Dutch rule of this part of the world. And the Dutch beat the English here.)

4. And create visual poetic art pieces out of those dusty fragments.

5. Rojas, Rick, "Centuries of New York History Prepare for a Move," New York *Times*, 5 January 2017, https://www.nytimes.com/2017/01/05/nyregion/new-york-documents-archives-records.html.

6. Geof Huth, Email to Society of American Archivist's Dictionary Working Group (5 January 2017).

7. Kate Bowers, Email to Society of American Archivists' Dictionary Working Group (5 January 2017).

8. New York, Arts and Cultural Affairs Law, § 57.05(4).

9. But not the records of the initial, the oldest, and the longest running of these branches of the Supreme Court of Judicature, because those were the records we held.

10. New York State, Laws of 1906, Chapter 661.

11. An office which fell under the administration of the City of New York at the time.

12. New York City, Local Law 70, 1941.

NECESSARY NOTHINGS

Although this story is a work of fiction, the very core of it actually occurred on the single day I was a reference archivist at the University at Albany. The story of Mr. Blumenthal, the man researching his own papers, the fact that he was using a fountain pen, the decision to allow him to continue, and his telling the archivist why he returned to his homeland all actually happened. His story still resonates within me.

MEMORY AND EVIDENCE

1. Hilary Jenkinson, "British Archives and the War," *The American Archivist*, 7:16 (January 1944).

2. David Bearman, "Archival Strategies," *The American Archivist* 58:4 (1995): 391.

3. William J. Maher, "Society and Archives," Incoming Presidential Address, August 30, 1997, in "Archives, Archivists, and Society," *The American Archivist* 61:2 (Fall 1998): 255.

4. William J. Maher, "Lost in a Disneyfied World: Archivists and Society in Late-Twentieth-Century America," Presidential Address, September 3, 1998, in "Archives, Archivists, and Society," *The American Archivist* 61:2 (Fall 1998): 262.

5. In my reminiscence here, I had written about an event in Pittsburgh, but Michael Knies, who was present at the event, later told me this had occurred in Bethlehem, Pennsylvania, which fact I recalled only after his reminder.

RECORDS AS OPPOSED TO ARCHIVES AS OPPOSED TO RECORDS

1. In this case, I mean the good appraisal archivist who examines a body of records without a conceived idea of how the appraisal will turn out. In appraisal, though, we almost always have the sense that the records may be archival—otherwise, we would have to carry out formal archival appraisals for each series of records created within our realm, no matter how obviously mundane and inutile each was.

2. When I first wrote this opening phrase, I ended it with solecism, which seemed definitely incorrect. Then I changed it to solipsism, and it was as if I, the archivist, had been transformed into a state of nothingness. Finally, I recalled syllogism. The human mind—bursting with so much information that it sheds torrents of it daily—can trick itself into believing something is factual without ever finding a fact to support that conclusion.

3. I desperately wanted to say conundra here (because of that untrue plural's goofiness in English), but conundrum is not even a Latin word. Etymologists believe it was a joke word created to approximate a term in Latin. ["conundrum, n.". OED Online. December 2018. Oxford University Press. http://www.oed.com.dbgateway.nysed.gov/view/Entry/40646?redirectedFrom =conundrum (accessed January 17, 2019).]

4. Bob Sink, "Episode 51: I Guess I Was Good at Osmosis," *An Archivist's Tale* (recorded 7 January 2019, posted 9 February 2019).

5. This is a reworking of Samuel Beckett's "I can't go on, I'll go on," from the end of the 1959 novel *The Unnamable*. I couldn't bear to make my version a comma splice, though.

6. Quoting directly here from Samuel Beckett's 1983 short story "Worstword Ho," which I have not read in decades.

REMEMBERING AS A FORM OF FORGETTING

1. This refers to Sir Hilary Jenkinson—for any non-archivists reading this. He was probably the most famous British archivist of all time.

2. However, it is possible to appraise records not yet created. Once, while working at the New York State Archives, we appraised a set of state government records as permanent and archival even though none of the records in that series had yet been created. A new law required the creation of a record and clearly described the purpose and required content of the record. Based on that provision, we determined these records would be born as archival records—and would not have to wait to be called such until they had reached middle age. I like to call such records born-archival records.

3. The babybook my mother kept about me, her first child, provides plenty of evidence of my breaking my nose at the age of almost three. However, I remember much more than the book indicates. As the only child, and a defiant one, not invited to a party in my neighborhood, I walked up the outside steel steps of a nearby apartment building to attend Katey Burton's birthday party. The children at the party, protected by a child safety gate at the top of the stairs yelled at me to go away, but I persisted in climbing toward them. When I reached the top, the flailing hands of the children disabled my balance, and I tumbled down the stairs, deviating my septum along the way. As a postscript, I was allowed into the apartment (part of graduate student housing for the University of California, Berkeley), where Katey's mother put me on the edge of her kitchen sink and cleaned the blood off me. All of these are details I recall from my remembered experience (except for Katey's name, which I know only because my parents sent the Burtons Christmas cards for decades after this event).

4. I'll note that the eldest child must have been no more than four years of age. I doubt I could have outrun anyone older than that. But I could run and climb. Those were my earliest profound skills.

5. Since first writing this, I've run across a record that I had my tonsils and adenoids taken out when I was one year and nine months old, and I recall sitting in bed and having ice cream brought to me afterwards. This is my earliest datable memory now, but a record allowed me to realize it was.

6. I remain a very shy man, but few who know me realize or recognize this, because I've taught myself how to overcome my shyness in professional situations, though a bit less so in personal and private ones.

7. One that may not need to be kept for long, since no-one or only a select number of people can ever see it.

8. Although I almost universally support the right of a people or nation to choose the name to call themselves (even the USA calling itself "America," as it has for centuries), I will not allow the Burmese the honor of their chosen name. A country so murderous toward their own people, one who will not even recognize the clear citizenship of their Rohingya minority deserves not the privilege to name itself.

9. Richard C. Paddock, "Aung San Suu Kyi Asks U.S. Not to Refer to 'Rohingya,'" New York *Times* (6 May 2016), https://www.nytimes.com/2016/05/07/world/asia/myanmar-rohingya-aung-san-suu-kyi.html.

10. Francis Buchanan, "A Comparative Vocabulary of Some of the Languages Spoken in the Burma Empire," *Asiatic Researches* 5 (1799): 219–240. But see also here: https://www.soas.ac.uk/sbbr/editions/file64276.pdf.

11. A person once revered for her bravery and resolve in the face of oppression—but this was before the world realized her interest in lessening oppression was based only on the fact that her people were being oppressed. Since she does not see the Rohingya as Burmese, she has no need to concern herself with their oppression, so she supports it instead. It is difficult for most humans to understand that we are all "of one blood" (Acts 17:26). Though I am completely unreligious, I recognize the scriptures of the world's religions can occasionally provide us with words to live by.

12. "Aung San Suu Kyi's Cowardly Stance on the Rohingya," Editorial, New York *Times* (9 May 2016), https://www.nytimes.com/2016/05/09/opinion/aung-san-suu-kyis-cowardly-stance-on-the-rohingya.html.

TO PRESERVE THE RECORD, PROTECT THE THREE M'S

1. That is, "Lots of Copies Keeps Stuff Safe," which produces the meaningful acronym LOCKSS. The latter is clearly a backronym, an acronym designed to be itself a word that repeats the meaning of the full term.

2. Well, they still do.

3. However, huge stores of unstable acetate blanket the planet, and many of these are slowly degrading through a process we call vinegar syndrome. Cold storage can stabilize this problem, but at greater cost. Worse still, nitrate microfilm still exists. It is a highly volatile base that can combust, giving it the means to destroy records beyond those it itself carries.

4. Though scent is an aspect we often hope to lose, not retain.

5. As a reminder, any digital object always exists in an actual physical location.

6. I originally created this concept of the 3 M's of preservation when I was traveling the U.S., training archivists on the basics of managing electronic records, but I eventually came to understand the concept encompassed records in any form.

7. I realize metadata is conceptually plural.

8. Note that I realize we usually divide metadata into three categories: descriptive (which tell us what the record is and what it contains), structural (which show how the records fit together and even how an individual record is internally organized), and administrative (which are used by custodians to manage the records, and which include preservation and intellectual property metadata). This framework is still a sound way to think about metadata. I'm just saying there's more than one way to divvy up metadata.

RECORD AS ORGANISM, RECORDS AS ECOSYSTEM

1. Geof Huth, *Appraising Digital Records* (Trends in Archives Practice, Module 14) in *Appraisal and Acquisition Strategies* (Society of American Archivists: Chicago, 2016).

2. After my departure from that job, the appraisal decision was overturned, apparently because of political considerations internal to my previous department of New York State. Certainly, managing such a system into the infinite would have been expensive—though my appraisal suggested sets of data to save, rather than recommending the indefinite maintenance of the whole shebang—and possible privacy concerns were also rampant, although confined to that slender subset of data for very small school districts (the smallest school district I have ever visited had a total student population of thirteen). Yet I still believe it a great loss to have abandoned this opportunity to understand the New York State educational system diachronically. It is always difficult to remove politics from government—but that is equally true in business and personal affairs.

3. Shirley Carvalhêdo Franco, "The Notion of Ramification of Archival Documents: The Example of the Fonds Related to the Brazilian Political Movement Araguaia Guerrilla," *The American Archivist* 78:1 (Spring/Summer 2015): 142.

4. These are, indeed, my own haplogroups, though there is not much genetic sleuthing you can do with this data.

5. My own country of origin and current residence being the one whose archival practices I best know.

6 To borrow a term I learned from Bill Maher, one-time president of the Society of American archivists and a good archival thinker. He used this term many times when my wife, Karen Jamison Trivette, and I were in Salamanca, Spain, last year for the joint meeting of the International Conference on Archives' Section for Research and University Archives (SUV) and the Conferencia de archiveros de las universidades españolas (CAU).

7. The word *collection* is one of those fraught (as I say) terms in archivy—an archival shapeshifter that might mean everything and nothing at once—though it's a tad less fraught than the term "archives" itself. In this sense, it means essentially what one would expect: things collected together, long after their original creation.

8. Though my archival, records management, and library responsibilities reach across the entire state and all of its 1514 courts, these archives are the primary focus of my archival activities.

9. This series continued to 1910, at which point the courts switched to a case file system of records management at the opening of a fiscal year, April the first. Earlier, on 1 July 1847, the Supreme Court had ceased to be a court of statewide jurisdiction and became a series of courts covering individual counties in the state. Since I am in the process of depatriating these records (transferring them to other entities), I have had to split this series so I could transfer these records to two different repositories: the first part to the New York State Archives and the second to the New York City Municipal Archives.

10. For instance, the general sequence of actions in an early civil case—alternating between the plaintiff and the defendant—is as follows: declaration (of the plaintiff), plea (or narratio, the defendant's reply to the declaration), replication, rejoinder, surrejoinder, rebutter, and surrebutter. The colony's and state's legal system was massively and unnecessarily complex until deep into the 19th century.

11. And they were shoved. Some boxes consist of nothing but unfoldered and fragmented documents piled atop each other, each bearing a penciled code applied to its backside.

12. I use "intended order" in place of "original order," because the latter often incompletely demonstrates itself, whereas the former accepts that order has an intent and that archivists should follow that intent whenever they can determine what it was—despite the "received order" of the records.

13. They encompass approximately 12,000 cubic feet.

14. Imposed order being any arrangement system created for a series after the active use of the series. Imposed order is always the domain of the archivist or of one serving as an archivist.

15. I realize that many people see zoos as animal prisons, and I appreciate and understand that point of view. However, we have at least a couple of reasons to support the practice of zookeeping: zoos allow people without the means to travel the world the opportunity to see live non-native animals and understand at least a portion of their form of beingness, and zoos give us a means to preserve the DNA of endangered animals, especially those highly poached animals of Africa.

16. Let alone value of an enduring sort.

AN ARCHIVIST'S TAIL: ARCHIVES AS SYMBOL

1. Or paper and pencil or toner, or acetate or nitrate or polyester and silver, or parchment and ink and wax, or digital bits and discs—or any number of other surfaces and surfacings.

2. He claimed the term *manufact* was an old term no longer used, but I have been unable to find any evidence of it anywhere except in his essay. My "dictionary entry" for the term follows the style guide of the Dictionary of Archives Terminology, and here it is:

> manufact
>
> n. ~ an artifact considered as an object that records and preserves meaning as an archival record does
>
> RELATED TERMS
>
> artifact
>
> manuscript
>
> muniment
>
> SYNONYM
>
> cognitive artifact
>
> NOTES
>
> Just as a manuscript is written by hand, a manufact is made by hand. Each is a human creation, each records the fact of its manufacture, and each transports meaning into the future for continued use by other humans. The concept of the manufact accepts that all "recordings" (even digital "recordings" of text or image or sound, or physical recordings in the form of objects) exist as physical realities that maintain information over time, thus each must be accorded the respect archivists usually reserve only for the record.
>
> CITATION
>
> Washburn, Wilcomb E. "Manuscripts and Manufacts," The American Archivist 27:2 (April 1964): 247. The important distinction is not between the written word and the material object but between the specific fact and the general idea. The specific fact may be either in the form of a written document—a manuscript—or a material artifact or "manufact" (if I may be permitted to use an archaic term to demonstrate the close relationship of the artifact and the manuscript). The historian has an obligation to the specific before he plunges into the general, and it is this responsibility that unifies the manuscript and the manufact.

3. The essay appeared in a book edited by H.L. Hix entitled *Made Priceless: A Few Things Money Can't Buy*. See here for said essayette on this object: 031454a.netsolhost.com/inquire/2012/12/06/geof-huth/.

4. Episode 43: 2X2: Our Retention Period is Permanent (Kerri Anne Burke and Alan Delozier), *An Archivist's Tale* (recorded 17 November 2018, released 15 December 2018).

5. James O'Toole, "The Symbolic Significance of Archives," *The American Archivist* 56:2 (Spring 1993).

LACUNAE INVISIBILITY, AND OTHER ARCHIVAL SILENCES

1. This was my friend Bob Grumman, who kept my voluminous paper correspondence to him in that car, along with other personal papers of his. The car didn't run, its tires were totally flat, but it rested in a carport, to give it a bit of protection from the elements. It survived a hit from a hurricane, for instance. I called the car the carchives. When Bob died, I (his literary executor) emptied the car and transferred its contents to his selected archives.

2. Geof Huth Papers 1960–2006 [but actually 1960–2020] (MSS-137). M. E. Grenander Department of Special Collections and Archives, University Libraries, University at Albany, State University of New York (https://library.albany.edu/speccoll/findaids/mss137.htm).

THE SLAVE REVOLT OF 1712

1. This essay was originally presented as a talk at the Archivists Round Table of New York's Archives Week Symposium held on 17 October 2019. I based that talk on an earlier one covering multiple stories from the archives of the New York County Clerk's Division of Old Records, which I presented at the Researching New York conference in Albany, New York, on 16 November 2018. That talk was entitled "The Courts as the Eyes of Culture: The Process of Dehumanization in Colonial New York," which was part of a session entitled "Coups from the Courts: The Historical Importance of New York's Legal Records."

2. You might be surprised, however, to learn that this court, operating under the simplified title Court of General Sessions, ceased operations only in 1962.

3. In this essay, as I did in the presentations that preceded it, I generally refer to enslaved people as "slaves" and to their enslavers as "slave owners." An attendee at the Archivists Round Table Symposium asked me if I was familiar with the contemporary practice of using the terms "enslaved person" and "enslavers" in place of the terms I used and also asked why I used the terms I did. I noted I was familiar with that practice and that I used these terms intentionally. I noted I used "slave" because it is unleavened, because it hurts me to say it, and because we need to feel pain when we discuss this grave injustice, the enslavement of other humans by our white predecessors. I explained I wanted to feel pain every time I said the word. I also noted that "enslaved person" feels like a euphemism to me, because "enslaved" does not feel as painful to me, and that is because nouns carry more weight than adjectives. I did not use the term "enslaved person" because the human element cannot be removed from the word "slave." To be a slave, one must be a person. I noted that, when I read the stories of these people, I always felt the horror of humans struggling to be free in the face of certain defeat and of their languishing towards death while hung, but not hanged, from a tree to die a drawn-out and excruciating death. I feel their humanity, I imagine their pain, and "slave" makes me feel those more sharply. Similarly, I did not use the word "enslaver," because "slave owner" is more painful to me. That term baldly identifies the fact that the laws and mores of our country allowed the legal ownership of humans—for centuries—so I use this term to dishonor those slaveholders, those people who believed they could own another person.

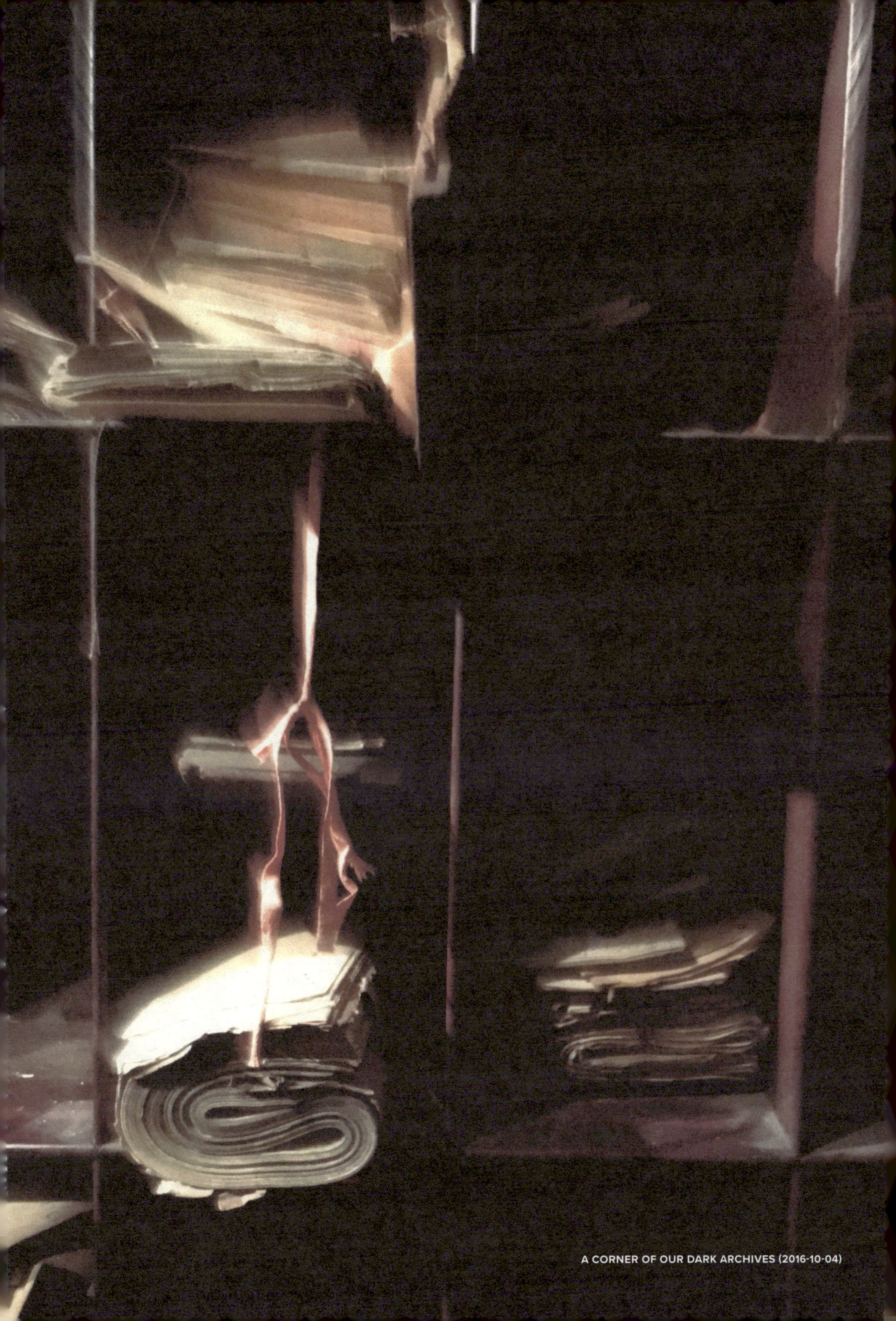

A CORNER OF OUR DARK ARCHIVES (2016-10-04)

The real issue is,

Are archivists trustworthy?

bell hooks, Talk at a session of the 2018 Archives Leadership Institute (Berea College: Berea, Kentucky, 22 June 2018).

#ALI18